SUMMARY

of the
Life
of

WALTER
CALDWELL
ROBINSON

by

MALCOLM J. WALKER

SUMMARY OF LIFE OF WALTER CALDWELL ROBINSON

Copyright 2025 © **Malcolm J. Walker.** All rights reserved.

ISBN 978-1-967362-47-9 (Paperback)
ISBN 978-1-967362-48-6 (Ebook)
ISBN 978-1-967362-49-3 (Hardcover)

Printed in the United States.

Contents

WALTER CALDWELL ROBINSON:
PRESIDENT AND LORD OF BLACK CHATTANOOGA

This book is lovingly dedicated in memory of my mother,
Nellie Walker-McReynolds; stepfather, Willie McReynolds;
siblings, Jacqueline McDuffie, Herschel Walker Jr.,
Nettie Humphrey, Ruth Sanderfur-Amaker;
and uncle, Victor Walker.

ACKNOWLEDGMENT

The writer is indebted to a number of people for making the completion of this study possible. He is earnestly grateful to the following: Mrs. Cora Robinson, wife; Ms. Marian Robinson, daughter; and Mrs. Evelyn Young, teacher in the Chattanooga School System, for directing him to associates of Walter Caldwell Robinson.

The writer also wishes to express special appreciation to Dr. Alonzo T. Stephens, his advisor and head of the Department of History, Political Science and Geography and professor of history; Ms. Lois C. McDougald, professor of history, for her guidance and constructive criticism; and Dr. George L. Davis, professor of history and political science, for his critique. A debt of gratitude is extended to these persons who were most helpful.

Sincere thanks and appreciation is also extended to numerous other persons who permitted interviews, who supplied information, or directed him to people who gave vital help in this study. The writer also wishes to thank his fraternity brother and friend, Judge Walter L. Williams, for encouraging him to publish this book.

For all mistakes of fact or interpretations and construction, the author accepts full responsibility.

INTRODUCTION

The contribution made by Walter Caldwell Robinson certainly deserves to be recorded and passed on to future generations. He played a very vital role in the black man's struggle in his city, state, and the nation. Robinson was responsible for lessening the burdens of thousands of black Americans and spent the majority of his life doing what often was thought impossible to get recognition and acceptance for his people as humans and first-class citizens.

The period in which Robinson struggled and the conditions under which he labored for black people was indeed challenging. The masses of black people during the 1920s-1950s in Chattanooga, Tennessee, were of the lowest socioeconomic status and possessed little educational training. Robinson organized blacks and spoke with power to whites because of his support from the black masses. He printed in his newspaper evils that were placed on blacks by whites and openly fought discrimination, segregation, and prejudice during a period when intimidation that would lead to lynching was about as common as prayer meetings and the Ku Klux Klan was as revered in the South as religion.

This great American would probably be forgotten in a few years if this study had not been undertaken. The writer is quite pleased to have had a part in capturing the activities of this great leader, politician, and businessman so that present and future citizens may profit from the contribution he made in Tennessee.

It was the purpose of this study to describe the life and activities of Walter Caldwell Robinson from 1893 to 1968. More specifically, it was the aim of this study to give an account of Robinson's early life as a farm boy in Alabama and in the ghetto of Chattanooga, Tennessee; to describe his efforts and successes in obtaining financial security; to present his activities as a politician, although he was never elected to a political office; to explain his contributions as a newspaper publisher and editor; and finally to summarize his major activities and contributions in his profession in a time when blacks were legally out of the accepted political arena.

This study is important because, to this date, nothing in the form of a biography or any other work has been written about this great citizen of Tennessee. This great American made life a little easier for blacks in Chattanooga as well as other areas of Tennessee and the nation. He organized black people for the purpose of electing white officials who would be considerate of the black man's problems. Believing that voting was the only sensible means of getting recognition during his time, Robinson put this means into action, and many accomplishments were made.

This study is biographical in nature, but political and business aspects are considered as they relate to the activities in which he was a part. Chattanooga, Tennessee, is the primary location, but other states and cities are mentioned as they relate to Robinson's activities.

The writer obtained data for this study primarily from the morgue and library of the *Chattanooga Times* and the *Chattanooga News Press*. Taped interviews with Robinson's relatives and associates proved to be most beneficial as primary information. Thus, on the whole, original and primary sources were used and interpreted.

CHAPTER I

Early Life

Joseph and Elizabeth Robinson were sharecroppers in Larkinsville, Alabama, on July 17, 1893, when Walter Caldwell Robinson was born. He was the fifth of seven children born to this couple. Being sharecroppers meant that their living conditions were the bare minimum. To supplement the family income, Elizabeth did the washing and ironing for whites in the community during the evenings, after having worked in the fields all day with her husband and children.

Realizing that the opportunity for improving their living conditions was virtually impossible in this community, the parents—Joseph and Elizabeth—decided to migrate to Chattanooga through the influence of Elizabeth's sister. Elizabeth's sister already lived in Chattanooga and realized that there were many opportunities in industry in the Chattanooga area that offered jobs with good pay for unskilled laborers. Also, there were educational facilities in Chattanooga that one could attend through high school.

When Walter was nine years old, the family moved to Chattanooga and rented a house on Thirteenth Street on the west side of town in an area called Tannery Flat. This community got this name because of a large industry there where leather was processed. Joseph was successful in securing a job in the Barkyard Tannery within walking

1

distance of their home. Elizabeth continued to do the laundry in her home for whites after moving to Chattanooga, Tennessee.

Walter and his brothers and sisters entered West Main Street Elementary School, although at that time it was called Montgomery Avenue School.

Even though Walter was nine years old upon arriving in Chattanooga, he had to start school as a first grader because in Alabama, he had not attended school regularly because he had to help on the farm, and the school he previously attended was not an up-to-date one. Walter excelled as a student and completed the eighth grade at the Montgomery Avenue location. Upon graduating from Montgomery Avenue, he entered Howard High School, then located on Eleventh Street. At Howard, Walter was an outstanding student and was selected to participate in many activities.

Walter was always an ambitious person and wanted very badly to help the family solve the financial difficulties. Thus, at the early age of about eleven years old, he managed to get a job in a plow foundry near his home as a "shake out man." Each morning before going to school, he would get up very early and report to the factory where various tools for plowing were made. There he would shake the finished products out of the molds that had been poured the day before.

Even though their living conditions improved somewhat after moving to Chattanooga, the Robinsons were still very poor. Walter often watched his mother wash and iron for the white families for many hours. After a while, he began to help her and became very good at this task himself.

When he was sixteen years old and yet a student at Howard High School, he opened Walter's Pressing Shop on the corner of Maple and Fourteenth. This shop was in the rear of a meat market that was run by a white man named Agnew. At the shop, Walter pressed men's suits and women's clothes. He was a very clean and neat person and felt that this business could be profitable if properly advertised and the work was done well. Walter had acquired the skill of doing excellent laundry work from helping his mother in years past. After a while, Walter's Pressing Shop grew into a very prosperous business. Walter was always a dedicated person and wanted to do whatever possible to help anyone in his race. One of the two employees he hired to help with the pressing had only one leg.

Walter grew more knowledgeable of the black man's many problems in Chattanooga as he listened to the older men, who would congregate at his pressing shop just to talk or to have their shoes shined by youngsters he had hired to shine shoes. His pressing business became so prosperous and demanding that he dropped out of Howard High School after completing two years of study. He then devoted his time fully to his new business.

Just down the street from him lived a beautiful young lady he had known since moving to Chattanooga. She attended the same school and became his sweetheart. Cora Adair was attracted to him because he was so dignified, respectable, neat, and considerate of others. It is therefore not unusual that Cora and Walter never dated anyone else.

Cora's parents were strict, as many parents were at that time, and their dates were limited to movies and attending church activities. Walter began to attend the church that Cora attended as a teenager and joined this church at age fifteen. This was the Second Missionary Baptist Church. Church was an important institution for blacks in Chattanooga.

Walter quickly emerged as a leader and became the president of the Baptist Young People's Union. The church was then located in the "Hollow" on Elm and Tenth.

In 1913, Walter and Cora were married in the home of Cora's parents. After marrying, they lived with Cora's parents, and he continued to operate the thriving business of his pressing shop as their means of livelihood. Later he became a molder at the plow factory where he had worked as a youngster as a shake out helper. He worked at the factory as well as operated his pressing shop. Thus engaging in two kinds of work. The work at the pressing shop was quite heavy on Thursday, Friday, and Saturday.

After being married two years, Cora's mother and father moved back to Sanford, Tennessee, in order that Cora's mother might care for her aging parents. They left the house in Chattanooga to Cora and Walter.

Walter was a good provider and struggled very hard to see that his family had most of the things it needed. Because of his belief that a father should be the provider for his family, Cora never worked, that is outside of the home.

To Walter and Cora were born seven children: Evelyn, Alma Lee, Marian, Jessell, Walter Jr., Camille, and Lucille—the latter twin girls.

The Robinsons were a very close family and enjoyed doing things together. On one occasion, they went to the auditorium to see Ella Fitzgerald. This was a grand occasion, and Walter and Cora were pleased to see their children so happily going back and forth to the concession stand, getting Cokes and popcorn and enjoying themselves so much. Ella was a great ballad singer who gained fame as the adopted daughter of the great Chick Webb, a band leader of the late 1930s, '40s, and early '50s. The Robinsons didn't live extravagantly but thoroughly enjoyed just doing little things together.

In 1928, when Walter and Cora were happily surprised with the birth of the twin girls, Camille and Lucille, Walter was so excited that he had the notice of their birth published in the *Chattanooga Times*. Walter invited people in from the street to show off his little girls.

Robinson, as can be noted in the success of his children, was a staunch believer in education. He often told his children that there were four things they needed; he would say, "Get some God in your heart, some sense in your head, some money in your pocket, and a ballot in your hand."

Evelyn received the BS and MS degrees from Tennessee A&I State University and is now a retired teacher from the Hamilton County School System in Chattanooga. Alma attended Tennessee A&I State University for two years, received LPN from Erlanger

Hospital, Chattanooga; laboratory technologist certificate from Beth Israel Hospital in New York, New York; and laboratory technologist certificate from Emory University, Atlanta, Georgia. She retired as a supervisor of laboratory technicians at Beth Israel Hospital in New York City. Marian received BS and MS degrees from Tennessee A&I State University and MS degree from University of Iowa. She did further study at Columbia University in New York. Marian retired from the Hamilton County School System of Chattanooga after teaching for thirty-two years. Walter C. Robinson Jr. received BS and MS degrees from Tennessee A&I State University and did further study at the University of Mississippi. He retired as Principal of a high school in Cleveland, Mississippi. Lucille received the BS degree from Tennessee A&I State University and did further study at Wayne University and received the MS degree from the University of Detroit, Detroit, Michigan. Camille received the BS and MS degrees from Tennessee A&I State University, did further study at University of Michigan, Ann Arbor, Michigan, and George Peabody College, Nashville, Tennessee. She retired as assistant professor in the Business Department of Tennessee A&I State University. Jessell only lived one year and three months.

There were many conditions involving the colored race that really troubled Walter. He remembered his mother telling him of his grandfather who was a slave in Alabama. His grandfather was an outspoken man who often was punished while a slave because he would slip off during the night and discuss with the slaves of the other cabins measures which could be taken to lessen the burdens of slavery. His grandfather was an organizer of people and used his every opportunity to plan and scheme to "outthink" the white masters. Walter also listened to the older men who discussed the plight of the colored race as they sat around his pressing shop. He felt that if his grandfather had the courage to attempt to do something about the situations as a slave, surely he could do something about the injustices, sufferings meted to the colored race during his lifetime as a free man.

City officials ignored the needs of the colored community. The streets were often unpaved, rough, and seldom repaired; health facilities and other conditions were bad. There were cases where a whole block would use one outdoor toilet and that without running water. The school facilities were not up to par, and there was hardly any lighting in the streets of this rather rough ghetto area.

Robinson began attending the political meetings held in his ward (Fourth Ward). He became very active and, at times, would have meetings to discuss with the people of his community the various problems facing them for the purpose of determining what they could do to solve these problems. The chairman of the Fourth Ward was a very old man named Hiram Tyree.

Because Robinson had been so active in the ward and so concerned about the people of the community, he was elected chairman of the ward, therefore dethroning Hiram Tyree, who had for years been the political czar of the Fourth Ward. The Fourth Ward was considered one of the most powerful Republican precincts in the South. It was estimated that this ward could swing a Republican majority of from approximately 1,200 to 2,000 votes in any election.

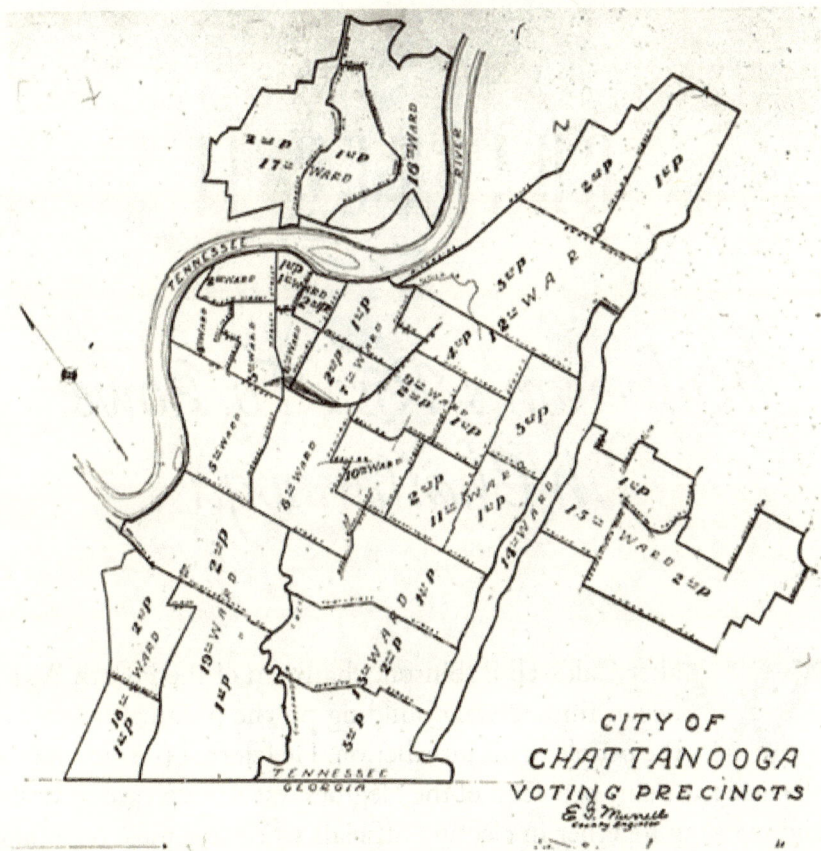

CHAPTER II

Robinson's Rise To Power In Chattanooga

Walter Caldwell Robinson, chairman of the Fourth Ward, began immediately building up the political interest of the people in his jurisdiction. He felt that the only way to alleviate the many problems of the Negroes was through group action and working together in electing officials who were most conscious of the Negro struggles.

First, he initiated a voter registration drive. He wanted every eligible voter of his ward to be registered, and he did his best to see that this was done. There were a number of people in the ward who could be depended upon to conduct door-to-door campaigns. He organized these concerned citizens, and every family in the Fourth Ward was visited. Those who were registered were encouraged to attend the instructional meetings, which were held once a month. Those who were not registered were strongly encouraged to do so.[3]

Robinson had built up quite a bit of interest in political affairs even before the first local election was held.

During the campaign period, he invited the various candidates to speak to the people of the ward and express their platforms or the things they intended to do. After all candidates had been heard, Robinson thought very seriously about which of them were the most sincere and which of them could be depended on to do the most for the colored race. He would then instruct the people of the ward as to who the best candidates were and those who should be supported at the polls. This procedure was used throughout his political career.[4]

Once candidates were in office, Robinson would ask them to do certain things that were within their power. He would ask favors for individual black people and for things that would benefit the entire black community. He asked for commissions and jobs for his followers in the various departments of city government.[5] He also approached these city officials concerning community development. He asked that streetlights be installed, that streets be repaired, and that proper sewage lines and connections be given attention in the area of the Fourth Ward. The residents of the Fourth Ward began to notice that some progress was being made, and this created more interest in political affairs.

Robinson started meeting with the chairmen and leaders of other black wards, and during elections, they began to work together in supporting certain candidates. The other leaders respected Robinson and his judgment; therefore, after a while, he was able to influence votes throughout all the black communities of Hamilton County.

White politicians began to notice the influence of Robinson and realized that he was significant in getting candidates elected.

In recognition of his oratorical ability and his rapidly rising political stardom, the National Republican Executive Committee invited him to conduct a campaign tour through a number of northern and northwestern states in 1926.[6] He accepted this offer and the newspapers in northern states gave him liberal space and praise.

Robinson was an excellent orator, and his commanding voice and diction caused ears to open as he captured the undivided attention of his audiences. He was also a staunch believer in the Republican Party. Even in personal letters to friends and relatives, he would praise the Republican Party and urge Negroes to cast their votes for Republicans as it was necessary to solve the problems of Negro people throughout the United States.[7]

The following is a portion of a speech delivered by Walter Caldwell Robinson in Richmond, Indiana, on October 26, 1956. In this speech, one will notice his confidence in the Republican Party.

Mr. Chairman and fellow Americans, it is good to be back in the great Republican state of Indiana to commune with you on the eve of this national election. As a citizen of Chattanooga, Tennessee, the home city of the Democratic nominee for Vice President, Senator Kefauver, I have elected to talk to you from a subject that I think is of great importance, not only to the Negroes of America, but the American people in general. Thus my subject, "THE RE-ELECTION OF DWIGHT DAVID EISENHOWER AND RICHARD NIXON AND A REPUBLICAN CONGRESS IS THE ONLY HOPE FOR NEGROES TO BECOME FIRST CLASS CITIZENS IN THE UNITED STATES OF AMERICA."

The choice between Eisenhower-Nixon and Stevenson-Kefauver must be made on November 6, 1956. Millions of American citizens will march to the polls on the date above mentioned to make their decision at the ballot box. But unfortunately, there are millions of Negroes in the deep South that will be prohibited from participating in this all-American election because the Democratic Party, who dominates and controls all of the southern states, and particularly those of the deep South, refused to permit Negroes to vote. Not by law, but by intimidation and intimidation is worse than by law.

The Democratic party is a party of disfranchisement, discrimination, and segregation and no party is entitled to be honored with the leadership of this nation who has built a reputation as a party who sponsors, believes and advocates segregation, discrimination, and non-compliance with the laws of the nation as enunciated by the justices of the Supreme Court of the United States.[8]

After Robinson toured the North and Northwest in 1926, the colored element of the Republican Party in the Third Congressional District insisted that their race was entitled to representation in the next National Republican Convention. Efforts were made to secure Robinson as an alternate. Many of the colored pastors and professional men of the district were especially active in backing Robinson.[9] It is important to note that Senator Kefauver was from Chattanooga and Robinson's own state.

The district was entitled to two regular delegates with full vote in the convention and two alternates who were to vote on the floor in the absence of the regular delegates.

In 1928, Robinson represented the Third Congressional District as an alternate delegate. This district was composed of Bledsoe, Bradley, Grundy, Dickerson, Hamilton, Marion, Meigs, Polk, Rhea, Sequatchie, Van Buren, Warren, and white counties in his state.[10]

In September of 1930, Robinson was the organizer of the Colored Voters League of Greater Chattanooga. The consensus of Robinson and the group initiating the Colored Voters League was that one of their most blessed privileges as American citizens in the state of Tennessee was their right of suffrage. Robinson had made colored citizens aware of the importance of organization and they were beginning to realize that public welfare depended upon political influence based upon voting strength. All the colored wards of Chattanooga therefore resolved to band together hoping to get what recognition they could.

The object and purpose of this organization was to inculcate and foster in the minds of its members, and the public generally, the importance of using their God-given right to cast a ballot in all elections, to teach obedience to law and order, to disseminate patriotism and loyalty to the government of the city, county, and states of the United States, and to assist their race in securing all the rights and privileges that other citizens of the United States enjoyed.[11]

Robinson was convinced that the best means of achieving any goal for the colored race was mass action with the ballot. In an address delivered at Spruce Street Baptist Church in Nashville, Tennessee, on February 16, 1958, he clearly explained his conviction that voting was a solution to the many problems of the colored race.

> You are sponsoring your program this year at a time when Negroes are going through the darkest periods in his history. The forces of darkness, led by irresponsible and uninformed people, have set up road blocks of hate to prevent the clear passage of Negroes from second class to first class citizenship. Especially is this true since the '54-'55 decisions of the Supreme Court of the United States. But Negroes are determined to become first class citizens in these United States of America. It can be done, it should be done, and it will be done providing that Negroes mass their action carrying with them their greatest protection, the ballot. Thus, my subject is MASS ACTION WITH A BALLOT IN HIS HAND IS THE WAY OUT FOR NEGROES.[12]

His Voters League was considered to be one of the most powerful political units in any state south of the Mason-Dixon Line.[13] Politicians interested in running for various offices in local elections usually contacted Robinson before deciding to run. They would do this because he was chairman of the Voters League and influenced votes of the entire black community. Robinson would listen to what they had to say, ask them questions, and then decide whether or not he would support them. In many instances, if he stated he would not support them, they declined to run because they knew that without Robinson, their chances of winning were hopeless.[14]

Even though Robinson was a staunch Republican, he sometimes supported candidates in local elections who were Democrats.[15] His decision on whether or not to support a Democrat in local elections depended on the ideas and character of competing candidates. Those whom he felt would be the most loyal to the cause of black citizens would be the ones supported.

The Colored Voters League was very active in the community. Each year the league sponsored a Lincoln-Douglass Program in

February. This fund-raising program was always informative. The lives of Abraham Lincoln and Frederick Douglas would be explained, and there would be an outstanding black person invited to speak. Music would be provided by local choirs and soloists.[16]

The Voters League also sponsored baby contests and other fund-raising activities. The funds raised from the Lincoln-Douglas celebration and other programs would be used to carry out activities of the league and to help people in distress.[17]

The league was credited with many achievements for the black race in Chattanooga. It continually asked politicians for favors that benefited colored individuals and the colored community as a whole. The league never failed to praise politicians for even any small deed for the black community.[18]

The Colored Voters League of Greater Chattanooga represented all the black communities of Chattanooga; therefore they could and would block vote and elect candidates of their choice. Politicians were afraid to deny the league's requests, which were feasible, just, and fair because they would not be reelected.

To give one example of the many activities that the league was involved in for the welfare of colored citizens, the following has been inserted. In 1933, the Colored Voters League of Greater Chattanooga sponsored a movement having as its object the placing of Negroes on the jury, especially in the cases where the fate of Negroes was involved. Many prominent white citizens of Chattanooga, including a municipal judge and the attorney general of the county, agreed with the black citizens in this movement.

This movement was sparked because of a trial in the first and second division of the criminal court of Hamilton County, involving a prominent high school student (black) who was charged with a serious offense and two young white men, Gross and Glover, who were charged with the murder of a black boy. The verdict returned by the jury in the above case where the colored student was given a sentence of life imprisonment and Glover was freed and Gross given a few years in the penitentiary.[19] The league based their strategy on the doings of other Southern cities. If there was something they wanted to ask the white politicians for, they would send a representative to other Southern cities to see if they had whatever was being asked for.[20] The league knew that Houston, Texas, a Southern city, had distinguished herself by placing Negro names on the wheel and strongly believed that Chattanooga should do the same. Their slogan was "'Tis sad justice knows no race, no color, and no religion—I wonder?"

In April of 1933 at the regular meeting of the Voters League, it was decided that the league would sponsor a motorcade to Dayton, Tennessee, on April 30, to attend the Congressional Convention. Also Walter Robinson and D. C. Harper (chairman of the Seventh Ward) were endorsed as alternate delegates to the Republican National Convention, which convened in June 1932 in Chicago, Illinois.

In 1934, a group of black leaders sent a letter to the chairman of the Executive Committee of the Republican Party stating why the black element of the Third Congressional District was entitled to representation on the State Republican Executive Committee. They offered the name of Walter Caldwell Robinson for election to that post in the coming August contest.[21]

On February 25, 1953, the Colored Voters League of Greater Chattanooga sent the following letter to Governor Clement:

Dear Governor:

The Pikeville Industrial School, located in close proximity to Pikeville, Tennessee, is a state institution, where incorrigible colored boys are sent for correction, has been a source of much concern of Negroes of Tennessee for a number of years.

We have been reliably informed that the boys in that institution have been and are now being mistreated in that some of the boys are hired out to individual farmers to help make crops. They are not being given adequate opportunities.

Therefore we respectfully urge that you correct that condition that exists at Pikeville, and we believe the best way to solve the problem is to appoint a qualified Negro as Superintendent of the institution, and we are certain that there are many qualified Negroes in Tennessee because the State of Tennessee appropriates millions of dollars a year to A. & I. State University to train Negroes.

We want to thank you in advance for your consideration of this matter.

Respectfully,
The Colored Voters League
of Greater Chattanooga
Special Committee:
/s
Walter C. Robinson
Rev. C. B. Holloway
Prof. J. W. Williams
Mr. Eugene Hyatt

Walter Robinson, now chairman of the Fourth Ward, chairman of the Colored Voters League of Greater Chattanooga, a member of the Republican's Speakers Bureau, and a member of the State Executive Committee of the Republican Party, was politically a very powerful man. Politicians throughout the state recognized him as a distinguished citizen. Because of this power and influence, Robinson was able to do many things for the black race throughout the state of Tennessee.

W. J. Hale and his successor, Dr. Walter S. Davis, presidents of Tennessee Agricultural and Industrial State College in Nashville, became close friends to Robinson because of Robinson's influence. He was in the position to ask the governor, legislators, and other influential politicians for grants and other appropriations for the college. Both Hale and Davis corresponded with Robinson regularly.[22] They both made a number of speeches in Chattanooga, having been invited by Walter Caldwell Robinson, and Robinson quite often was a guest on the campus of Tennessee Agricultural and Industrial State College.

On occasions, Robinson would ask favors of Hale and Davis. These favors usually concerned privileges for students from the Chattanooga area. Following is an example of letters to President Davis asking for such privileges.

The Chattanooga Observer

Post Office Box 293

Chattanooga, Tennessee

December 30, 1953

Dr. W. S. Davis, President

A. & I. State University

Nashville, Tennessee

Dear Dr. Davis,

I am writing you relative to one Johnny Russell, who is a freshman in your school and lives at 2815 Long Street, Chattanooga.

His father, Willard Russell, the District Manager of the Union Protective Assurance Company here, is meeting with some financial difficulty and he is interested in his boy remaining in school. He feels that if the boy can get some work at your university it will help him greatly and insure the boy's stay in the University.

I understand the boy is not on the campus but lives in the city and he says it is more expensive to live off the campus, but at the time he was accepted in the school there was no dormitory space for him. Please see what you can do for him and I will appreciate it. I think if we can help him it will prove mutually beneficial to all concerned.

Thanks in advance for the consideration that you will show Johnny Russell.

I have been so busy since I returned to Chattanooga from your city during the dedication of your buildings there that I haven't had the time to express to you my appreciation for everything done for me while in your city. Your program was ideal and I've heard nothing but compliments on your work from all over the country.

May I wish for you and yours continued good health, happiness and prosperity during the new year. I remain . . .

Your sincere Well-Wisher

/s

Walter C. Robinson

Walter Caldwell Robinson was a deeply religious man, and from the time he joined Second Missionary Baptist Church in his youth until his health failed in old age, Robinson worked faithfully for the church. He became a trustee in the church at about the age of twenty-one years and held that position until his death.

Robinson's political involvements also were of benefit to his church. In 1921 when Second Missionary Baptist Church was relocated, he was successful in getting from city officials in Chattanooga enough rock, cement, and sand and other materials necessary to build the basement of the church. This donation was worth thousands of dollars.[23] He was active in fund-raising activities and would ask politicians and wealthy whites for money for church undertakings.[24]

Robinson was also instrumental in getting pastors for the church. Second Missionary Baptist Church, for various reasons, had a long list of pastors. Rev. M. H. Ribbins, one that was loved and respected by the members very much and remained a pastor for sixteen years until his death, was secured as pastor for the church by Walter Caldwell Robinson.[25]

In 1966, the Second Missionary Baptist Church presented Robinson a trophy with the following inscribed on it: "In appreciation of your many years of service—Officers and Members of Second Missionary Baptist Church—348 Grove Street."

Robinson was also active in several civic organizations as well as fraternal societies. He was chairman of the colored division of the Community Chest. (This organization was similar to the United

Fund Campaign of today.) He was a member of the American Woodmen, which was a fraternal organization, and for twelve years, he served on the Better Housing Commission.

Robinson supported H. D. Huffacker for city commissioner of education in the local election of 1927. Huffacker was elected and, during the same year, hired Robinson as a truant officer. He was given an office in the city hall from which to work. Robinson worked diligently under Huffacker and commanded the respect of whites at city hall as well as colored students and teachers throughout the city of Chattanooga.

Robinson continued to be very active in politics, and having a job as a truant officer gave him the opportunity to visit homes and discuss politics with parents and invite them to attend ward meetings. He also came in contact with teachers who were willing to cooperate with his requests because he was very powerful in the Department of Education.

Whenever Robinson visited a school, the principal and teachers displayed their very best professional abilities because they respected and feared Robinson as they would the superintendent of schools because of his power.[26]

Robinson was one of the most powerful men at city hall. Every person there holding a political job needed to be friendly with him because he had the power to get them out of office at election time. Because of his power, his job as a truant officer extended far beyond its description. Robinson had the power to hire and fire colored teachers.[27]

To further prove that Robinson was in the position to see that colored teachers were employed, the following letter written by Mrs. Mary L. Carter, dated November 11, 1934, is included as follows:

My Dear Mr. Robinson:

I am writing this, a message of appeal, and sincerely hope you will accept it in the spirit in which it is written.

I was in the City Hall twice, yesterday and today, but failed to locate you.

I am asking that you do what you can toward getting me placed in the City School System.

There is a vacancy now and I believe you could get me placed if you so desired.

I want to assure you here, which assertion may be used at any future date, that I will be responsible for any action or misunderstanding in the future, that may have any tendency to cause you, or anyone instrumental in giving me employment to feel that we are loyal, or that we would dare to "bite" the hand that feeds us.

Please do whatever is in your power for me, and count my father and me among your loyal supporters in whatever way we may be of service.

Thanking you in advance for your kind consideration.

I-am-Very truly,
/s
Mrs. M. L. Carter
(Rev. E. Moore)

CHAPTER III

President and Lord of Black Chattanooga

On January 26, 1933, Commissioner H. D. Huffacker died. A few days later, Walter R. Kendrick, a colored leader, in a statement to the *Chattanooga Times*[28] stated that Walter Robinson, Negro truant officer employed by the City Department of Education, is a "burden of oppression" to the colored citizens of Chattanooga. Kendrick declared that the truant officer does nothing but "build and repair his political machine."

Kendrick said that for six years colored people have been carrying this burden and they are saying,

> I shall not carry it further. The colored citizens of Chattanooga are entitled to a colored truant officer to look after our boys and girls and keep them in school instead of letting them run at large through the streets.

> Kendrick continued, I know that these citizens are willing to pay taxes for such a worthy cause, but these same citizens, and I may add the entire public, are taxed $1,888 per year plus expenses for a truant officer, then this officer does nothing but build and repair his political machine for his own selfish purpose.

He charged that the officer keeps up his political machine by oppressing school teachers and janitors of Chattanooga and leaves our little boys and girls out in the streets and dives of the city.[29]

Kendrick declared that Robinson had a monopoly on all school buildings, parks, and playgrounds and charged that no one could secure the accommodations of these public places without paying a fee unless the applicant was a member of the Colored Voters League of Greater Chattanooga, of which he is the "President and Lord."

He said that Robinson had "let out" the Second District school building to a preacher of the Fourth Ward for church services for twelve months and that this preacher was one of Robinson's lieutenants.

Kendrick said that lights, coal, and janitor services were being furnished at the expense of taxpayers.

"The public," Kendrick said, "is anxiously waiting to see what will be the status of Robinson since Commissioner Huffacker's death, and there is a possibility of Chattanooga having a new Commissioner of Education. Will the new commissioner tolerate Robinson's activities? No, I think not. Mr. Commissioner, whoever you may be, please give us relief from conditions which have existed in the Department of Education for six years."[30]

Another commissioner was elected in March of 1933, and for a while, it was not certain what position he would take regarding Robinson. Of course Robinson was a very astute man and was familiar with every phase of politics.

Robinson held a Fourth Ward meeting shortly after W. E. Wilkerson was elected, which was devoted mainly to boosting Commissioner W. E. Wilkerson, Robinson's new employer, as head of the City Department of Education.[31]

Commissioner Wilkerson was not present to address the four hundred Negroes who filled the church at Fourteenth and Sycamore Streets, but Robinson and colored supporters spoke on behalf of Mr.

Wilkerson, who became school commissioner unexpectedly upon the death of Commissioner H. E. Huffacker.

One of the reasons given by Robinson for support of Wilkerson was the statement by Professor T. H. McMillan that if he should be elected to succeed Huffacker, one of his first acts would be the discharge of Robinson, who was Negro truant officer for the city schools.[32]

On September 28, 1933, Mayor Ed Bass made an announcement through Superintendent W. T. Robinson's office that three employees of the Department of Education, including Boyd Hargraves, a white referee of compulsory attendance, had been fired due to the effects of the Depression. Walter Robinson, Negro politician, employed under the title of attendance officer, who was directly under Mr. Hargraves and who drew a salary of $135 a month, was still retained. Mr. Hargraves received $50 a month, although he formerly drew $150 before the Depression.[33]

There were a number of complaints that Robinson dominated the Chattanooga School System and that politics was a major problem affecting the entire system. A letter appeared in the *Chattanooga Times* stating that

> the colored ministers of Chattanooga do hereby respectfully and enthusiastically endorse Walter Robinson and the work he is doing. He is always trustworthy and dependable and a cleancut christian gentleman and taxpayer.

> The statement was signed by a number of ministers.

The Colored Ministers Alliance replied to this letter in the *Chattanooga Times* the very next day, stating that

> it voices its strongest protest and disapproval at the assertion made in that newspaper that the colored ministers of the city endorsed the activities of an employee of the Department of Education. This assertion, they said was erroneous, misleading and greatly unfair to the ministers of their city as a whole.

> We as Negro ministers, stand squarely and solidly for the absolute divorcement of politics from our schools. We are convinced that

for the sake of our children, our teachers, our citizenry, our schools should and must be free. To this end we shall unceasingly labor, giving gladly our full cooperation to all who share this high purpose.[34]

W. E. Wilkerson, the new commissioner of education, in a talk before the black teachers at Howard High School said the following:

Teachers need not have any fear about their positions so long as they did their work and gave loyalty to the department. They did not have to join anything to secure or hold their positions. That no teacher can give the best of service under the conditions of fear. I am glad that freedom has come to our teachers, who for six years have been harassed, humiliated and exploited by the self-styled political boss of the Fourth Ward. Now that they have been liberated from this exacting and heartless ruler I congratulate them for their courage and patience. I believe this will bring a new day in the educational efforts of every teacher to the end that our children will enjoy the benefits of contact with satisfied and conscientious instructors.[35]

There were a number of black teachers and leaders who were pleased with Wilkerson's stand. They felt that the commissioner was referring to the Colored Voters League of Greater Chattanooga when he stated that teachers did not have to join anything to hold their jobs. William E. Thornhill was one of those colored people who praised the commissioner. He said that too much praise cannot be said of Wilkerson. "I wish him the most outstanding administration in his efforts to put the public schools of Chattanooga in the fore front."[36]

A group of black pastors, shortly after W. E. Wilkerson became commissioner, charged that Walter Robinson had influenced the selection of colored teachers as well as having a hand in fixing their salaries. A representative of the news sought to investigate these charges that politics rather than qualifications governed the amount of pay received by teachers. Wilkerson declined to release the salary list of colored teachers to the news representative.

I think the salary of a teacher is a private contract and I see no reason why I should let anyone see the salary list the new commissioner stated.[37]

Of course I would fire Walter if he did anything wrong, but nothing has come to me officially or privately that would show that he has been guilty of misconduct.[38]

Commissioner Wilkerson stated, I don't believe he would be so crude as to try to "shake down" teachers or fix their pay. He further stated that he asked several colored teachers if Walter had anything to do with their appointment or salary and all said that he did not. No one has been able to give me any proof that he has attempted to exercise control over the teachers or schools. In fact, most of the ministers who have talked to me have endorsed Walter's work.[39]

He expressed the opinion that Robinson has aroused the enmity of certain groups in city hall, which he was not supporting, and that Negro factions opposed to Robinson are envious of him. W. R. Kendrick, the Negro who has been assailing Robinson, is a "red," Commissioner Wilkerson declared.

The fact is Robinson is industrious and efficient. He is busy all the time and he makes daily reports to me showing how many schools he has visited, the number of truants returned to school, why he has not returned others and the number of parents he has interviewed. His reports show that he is doing a good work along this line.[40]

W. R. Kendrick released the following statement to the *Chattanooga Times* on October 9, 1933:

We, the public, had hoped that in Commissioner Wilkerson we had found a friend who was willing to assist us in a generous way in cleaning up the Department of Education, but from his interview with the news reporter it seems that he, too is afraid of Walter and is looking forward to Walter for 3,000 votes in 1935. Of course, Mr. Wilkerson, Walter will never be able to deliver to you 1,000 votes during 1935.

Now quit pussyfooting and let the public know where you stand. I don't have anything personal against Walter; I don't want his job, but you know, Mr. Wilkerson, that there is quite a bit of politics in the Negro school system.

Why didn't you tell the news reporter about the charges which I placed on your desk March 3, 1933? Your talk and consideration of me were very courteous; you impressed me as strictly a man of business and you assured me that you would go into the matter thoroughly. I gave you names of some of the most reputable white citizens of Chattanooga. I also gave you names of the leading manufacturers of Chattanooga and White civic organizations for references. Mr. Wilkerson, there is not a man or woman living or dead who can say that I am "red." My life is an open book, if you or any other man can prove to any fair-minded jury that I am a "red" or that my activities have been as such I shall never say another word against the department of which you are commissioner.[41]

W. R. Kendrick and a group of black pastors were successful in bringing before the public a lot of criticism, some truth and some propaganda, involving Walter Caldwell Robinson and the city school system. The public was becoming concerned, and many felt that W. E. Wilkerson should not be reelected as commissioner of education.

T. H. McMillan had made the statement in 1933 when W. E. Wilkerson was elected to succeed Huffacker that if he was elected, he would fire Walter Robinson. During local election of 1935, McMillan ran against Wilkerson for the post of commissioner of education. One of the things that McMillan promised the voters was that he would rid the public schools of politics.

In March of 1935, about nine thousand citizens of the city of Chattanooga went to the polls and voted for and elected T. H. McMillan for the post of commissioner of education.[42]

One of the first things Commissioner McMillan asked to see when he took office following the inauguration was Robinson's written resignation. It had been handed to Mr. Wilkerson a few days before forestalling dismissal that had been promised by the new commissioner.[43]

The resignation reads as follows:

Dear Mr. Commissioner:

Please be advised that I hereby tender my resignation as attendance officer in the department of education, effective at once.

For about eight years I have had the honor and privilege of serving the department of education in the city of Chattanooga as attendance officer and during all this time, in my humble way I have in good faith sought to do my duty.

For a little over two years, I have had the pleasure of serving under you, and may I take this occasion to say that you have accorded me fair treatment and every encouragement in my work as attendance officer. All this I appreciate more than I can express.[44]

T. H. McMillan was not really concerned about the black community as far as sound education was concerned but was determined to dethrone Walter Caldwell Robinson and openly pursue his allies. The very first day in office, McMillan released to the newspapers a report stating that Walter Robinson received from the city $400 for filing with the department one report, so far as all visible evidence revealed.

Robinson left behind him as a record of his work for the first four months of 1935 one report filed January 15, concerning the activities of his office, in addition to his resignation addressed to former Commissioner Wilkerson. Commissioner McMillan declared so far as he had been able to learn, "Robinson had not turned in an attendance report since January 15, and that was the only one he had made in 1935."[45]

McMillan began immediately to harass teachers and janitors who were known to be loyal to Walter Robinson. The headlines of one of the two major newspapers in Chattanooga read as follows: "GIVE COLORED CHILDREN SQUARE DEAL SAYS MCMILLAN" on September 26, 1935.[46] McMillan charged that Walter Robinson had hired a number of incompetent teachers. Actually, these were the teachers McMillan knew to be friends of Walter Robinson.

Paralee Shropshire was accused of having conduct not becoming to a teacher as well as being incompetent. The case was carried to trial, and Shropshire won. Clara Mae Frierson was an accomplished musician and a trained pianist and singer who happened to have been a classmate of Walter Robinson's. McMillan let the axe fall on this teacher and secretary. She and her attorney, John H. Early, charged that she was dismissed without notification of charges against her.[47]

"She's Walter Robinson's friend—that's the political reason behind the commissioner's unfair treatment of her," Attorney Early asserted. Clara Mae Frierson taught at the Main Street School for three terms, 1913-1915. She left Chattanooga to study music in Chicago and then had a professional career before going to Detroit to direct music and teach at the Community Union. She returned to Chattanooga and, last year, was employed at the Second District School as special music teacher assistant to Principal J. G. Vaughn.[48]

That year, Vaughn, also a Robinsonite, was fired, and George A. Key, formerly of Howard School, was given the job.

> I was told nothing about being dismissed, the ousted teacher said. I reported for duty Friday and was informed by Professor Key to call the Superintendent of schools. The Superintendent (W. T. Robinson) told me that I had been dismissed and that Commissioner McMillan had placed Marion Bynes in my place. Superintendent Robinson was not able to give Clara Frierson any reason for her dismissal.[49]

There were a number of other teachers and janitors dismissed by McMillan. Some took their cases to court and won, and others did not.

Commissioner McMillan continued to insult Robinson every chance he got. In 1938, Commissioner T. H. McMillan informed board members that the time had come when the Westside Colored School must have a name and suggested, "The James A. Henry

School in honor of the first principal of Howard High, Colored." There was silence, then Mayor E. D. Bass spoke, "Gentlemen, I should like to present the name of a prominent colored citizen who possibly has done more for his race than any one person... Walter C. Robinson, for the honor." Commissioner McMillan looked up in astonishment. Then someone, not Commissioner McMillan, laughed, and unable to restrain himself any longer, the mayor joined and finally McMillan himself. The school was then duly named for Principal Henry, and the commissioner of education so instructed to have it carried out on the cornerstone.[50]

Walter Caldwell Robinson, for a while, lost some of his power due to all the bad publicity by McMillan, W. R. Kendrick, and a group of black pastors. Their propaganda spread wide and had its effect especially during the election year of 1935.

The black community realized after a short period that McMillan was not really concerned for the plight of the black school children or the black race in general. It became obvious that he was just a politician determined to humiliate Walter Caldwell Robinson for opposing him.

Finally, Robinson managed to rebuild the confidence of most black citizens, and his political machine became as powerful as it had been before.

Walter Caldwell Robinson's leadership was put to a test in August 1936 involving a referendum for bonds. The people were asked to approve $100,000 library bonds; $20,000 school repair bonds; $140,000 fire alarm system bonds; $119,400 sewer bonds; $110,000 park and playground bonds; $21,250 airport bonds; $5,000 golf bonds; $600,250 market house bonds; $15,000 comfort station bonds; and $300,000 hospital bonds.[51]

Robinson took the position in the fight that to issue the amount of bonds asked for would necessitate an increase in tax rate. Because of unemployment and the overburdened tax payers, to tax them further, he felt, would be an imposition. His opposition composed of the same gang with few exceptions that had fought him for many years.

They took the position that all the bonds should be issued, and they were for every one of them. The coalition tried desperately to defeat Robinson in his own ward, the famous Fourth. They were ably assisted by the commissioner of education, who sent scores of teachers in Robinson's ward to canvass it from door-to-door, for ten consecutive days prior to the election. They had rallies in the Fourth Ward with the commissioner of education speaking, who promised to give them a $190,000 school building in the Fourth Ward. They distributed literature in great quantities. They gave out statements through the press boastingly that Robinson wouldn't carry his own ward.[52]

The white political enemies of Walter Caldwell Robinson tried to use their old fear tactics during the campaign for the bonds. One night while the family was sleeping, loud noises were heard, and Mrs. Robinson went to the door to see what was happening. She noticed a band of hooded Ku Klux Klansmen coming onto their porch with a casket. She naturally was frightened, and her fear spread to the children, who were awaken by now and were screaming and crying. Robinson got out of bed to see what the trouble was and noticed they were about to place the casket on the porch. He went to the door and ordered them to leave his property. He then went into the house and telephoned the grand wizard of the Ku Klux Klan. Being a very knowledgeable person of all powerful units of the city, he also knew the leader of the Klansmen. He asked the wizard why his people were parading around his house. The leader explained that he did not know anything about their activities there but assured Robinson that this would not happen again.[53]

When the battle was over and the smoke cleared away, Robinson won handsome majorities against issues in the Fourth Ward.

The white press and influential white citizens conceded that Robinson's activities contributed to the defeat of several of the bonds, particularly the library. Those who knew the political games concluded that it was a great victory for Robinson and for him to have won his point and carried his ward over the serious opposition that he had was nothing short of a miracle.

Robinson continued to be a very powerful politician in the Chattanooga area until his ward was split up in 1959 due to urban renewal. He was an alternate delegate to the Republican National Convention each year until his health failed.

CHAPTER IV

Robinson: editor and publisher

Walter Caldwell Robinson experienced some adverse publicity through the newspapers of Chattanooga, Tennessee. Not only had city officials attempted to smear his name but some black citizens with whom he had worked very closely, such as W. R. Kendrick and a small group of black pastors, attempted to curb his reign as the top black politician.

Robinson realized that the whites had the advantage over him in getting space in the local newspapers for the purpose of expressing their views. He was very troubled with the effect this publicity was having on his position. Because of fear, many of his friends, who held government-controlled jobs, were afraid to openly talk to him and dared not be seen with him, especially after T. H. McMillan became commissioner of education. These friends realized their jobs would be lost and chose to pretend not to be his friends. Even the teachers, janitors, and other city employees who Walter helped get employed refused to be seen with him, thus producing a type of loneliness that often comes to politicians.

Not only was Robinson plagued with the idea of bad publicity but also with the fact that the majority of the blacks were not aware of the many terrible deeds that were taking place that directly or indirectly involved the black citizens in his city, state, and the nation.

Robinson searched and searched for a way to express his opinions openly and squarely in a way that the majority would hear. His search included the desire to inform his people of the conditions that existed in hopes that they would become concerned enough to mass their action and solve some of the many problems. He searched for a way to reach the entire black community in order to let those who were too apathetic to attend the ward meetings or the meetings of the Colored Voters League of Greater Chattanooga know of the activities of these organizations and the reason for support of candidates they supported who Walter felt were for the good of all the blacks. After much thought and deliberation, he came upon the idea of a newspaper of his own.[54]

A black newspaper, the *Chattanooga Defender*, had been published in Chattanooga but had gone out of business when the publisher died. The publisher was a very outstanding Chattanoogan whose name was J. J. J. Oldfield.[55]

In 1933, Walter Caldwell Robinson initiated a newspaper, which was called the *Chattanooga Observer*. The editor and publisher opened an office at 208 East Ninth Street in the heart of the gateway city of the South (Chattanooga, Tennessee).

Robinson realized that publishing a newspaper was not an easy task. First of all, he decided that because he had no knowledge of printing himself and hiring a printer plus buying the equipment could be very expensive, he decided to get in touch with the Scott Newspaper Syndicate in Atlanta, Georgia, which did the printing for several black papers, such as the *Birmingham World* and the *Memphis World*. C. A. Scott, the general manager of the Scott Newspaper Syndicate, and Robinson were successful in making an agreement.[56]

The Scott Newspaper Syndicate in 1943 charged Robinson $13.25 for printing the first two hundred copies of an eight-page paper. For additional copies, $1.80 per hundred up to two thousand copies, and $1.40 per hundred for additional copies over two thousand.[57]

Composition costs $1.15 per galley; new ads, ten cents per inch; reruns, five cents per inch; for special front-page makeup, $3.50;

for extra makeup in excess to three pages and changes on the front, sports, and editorial pages, an additional charge at the rate of $1.75 per page.[58]

Casts for one inch cost fifty cents; two columns were seventy-five cents; three were ninety cents; four were $1.00, and five columns were $1.10. Cuts were $2.00 for one column; for two columns, $3.90; for three columns, $4.50, and for five columns, $5.75. For larger sizes, $1.25 was to be added for each column. Robinson sold the papers for six cents each in 1943.

Robinson's advertising rates in 1965 were eight cents per line or one dollar ($1) per inch. For five thousand lines, a reduced cost of six cents per line, and ten thousand lines were only five cents per line.[59]

8 CHATTANOOGA OBSERVER ● Friday, April 3, 1964

CHATTANOOGA OBSERVER

Published Every Friday at 208 East Ninth Street
Chattanooga, Tennessee
BY THE NEGRO NEWS PUBLISHING COMPANY

WALTER C. ROBINSON _____ Manager

SUBSCRIPTION RATES

1 Year — $5.50   6 Months — $2.75   3 Months — $1.38
Ten Cents Per Copy

Telephone: AM 6-0861   P. O. Box 292
Entered as Second-class Mail Matter February 1951 at U. S. Post
Office, Chattanooga, Tennessee.

Ike At The Mike

Newscaster Dwight David Eisenhower will add a new dimension to political reporting this summer when he assists the American Broadcasting Company in covering the Republican National Convention.

(ABC has secured the former President for spot appearances in the role of analyst.)

The logical next step is for the National Broadcasting Company or Columbia to sign peppery Harry S. Truman as the Democratic expert for the Atlantic City conclave.

The unique insight which past presidents would be able to give the American public would add to our political education. Television has made it possible for all of us to be arena spectators at the great American spectacles. If former Presidents (and Vice Presidents) and high party officials are enlisted to comment on, and explain, behind-the-scenes battles waged during conventions, it will be in the public interest.

In The Best Of Humidors

By SAMUEL McKINLEY LEVINE

There is a box
without locks
Is my tobacco.
My pipe I fill
To get
A smokey thrill
From my tobacco.
It takes
More than a broom
To clear the room
of the smoke
From my tobacco.
The smoke
May be strong
And I
May be wrong
So—
I load up my pipe
And fill the room
That takes
More than a broom
To clear
The smoke
From my tobacco.

(Copyright claimed by the author)

The question is, "To kill or not to kill?"

Is murder and suicide—slow and painful—a licensed privilege?

The tobacco interests claim "a reasonable doubt as to the deathly effects of tobacco." Is there any doubt about tobacco's lack of contribution to the betterment of one's health?

The tobacco industry's chief claim to survival seems to be centered on the economy.

Our federal health department gives posted advice to protect the health of the nation's people.

Regardless of which is more potent, cigarettes, pesticides, nuclear fallout or political fallout: Should we not forbid the sale of all tobacco products to minors in the age of 16? And should we not rigidly enforce the law? ? ?! !

Jacksonville Police
Scandal Mushrooming

Chattanooga Distr
Life Ins. Co. Wins 1

From boarding the train Saturday night for an anticipated night's rest in pullmans to attend the Annual Conference in St. Louis at the Marian Union Hotel to the return flight by Eastern Air Lines, Thursday afternoon, we were moved by the spirit of the great N. B. Herndon; "Nothing but the best is good enough for Policyholders and employees of the Great Atlanta Life Insurance Company."

The Chattanooga District won a plaque for having on its staff one of the best supervisors in the com-

pany system. The th representing the Chattrict as pictured above L. Watson, Manager; 1 pervisor; D. S. Bryson, brought back to Ch beautiful "trophy" was trict for outstanding performance. This is the first the operation of Atl Chattanooga the Distr is housed with the trip to the National World's Fair.

The theme of the C

CHATTANOOGA OBSERVER   6   Friday, June 14, 1963

CHATTANOOGA OBSERVER

Published Every Friday at 203 East Ninth Street
Chattanooga, Tennessee
BY THE NEGRO NEWS PUBLISHING COMPANY

_____ C. ROBINSON _____ Manager

SUBSCRIPTION RATES
Year—$3.12   6 Months—$1.60   3 Months—85 Cents
Ten Cents Per Copy

_____ P. O. Box ___

I COVER THE TOWN

By Peter D. Simmons

We Need Help?

● CHATTANOOGA OBSERVER ● Friday, June 21, 1963

CHATTANOOGA OBSERVER

Published Every Friday at 208 East Ninth Street
Chattanooga, Tennessee
BY THE NEGRO NEWS PUBLISHING COMPANY

WALTER C. ROBINSON _____ Manager

SUBSCRIPTION RATES
1 Year—$3.12   6 Months—$1.60   3 Months—85 Cents
Ten Cents Per Copy

Telephone AM 6-0813   P. O. Box 293

Entered as Second-class Mail Matter February, 1955 at U. S. Post-office, Chattanooga, Tennessee.

Find Medgar Evers' Slayer, Crush The Cause He Represented

The ambush slaying of Medgar W. Evers, 37-year-old Mississippi NAACP field secretary, brings anguish and shame to the nation. That he should die, through such an act of barbarity and cowardice, reflects the temper and times of Mississippi, in the face of this nation's struggles to make democracy a reality for all.

Evers' sacrificial death, while simply in the commission of an act to rid his native state and the nation of its cancerous, subhuman sores, should have wide effect on the nation. It is shocking and regrettable. Even Mississippians who opposed the NAACP freedom program there were quick to deplore his murder. The President of the United States said he was "appalled" by the crime, just outside Evers' home.

We hope that the killer or killers of Medgar Evers will be found and prosecuted to the letter of the law. It is commendable that the NAACP quickly offered $10,000 for the arrest and conviction of the assassin. The city of Jackson posted $5,000, the United Steelworkers Union $5,000, the American Guild of Variety Artists $1,000 and the Jackson, Miss., newspaper $1,000 within hours after the dastardly act. Undoubtedly, others will add to the rewards totalling $22,000 the first day, for the crime is so reprehensible that it must be solved, even in the angry climate of Jackson, Miss.

Those seriously working to clarify and guarantee civil rights for every citizen in the nation will take the Evers' murder as the signal for increasing their dedication and zeal for the righteous cause. He must not have died in vain!

The President Was Forthright In His Speech; Now, Let Congress Face Up To The Challenge

Prefacing one of the greatest civil rights plans in history, President John F. Kennedy told the nation over a TV-Radio hookup that it faces a moral crisis as a result of the rising tide of Negro discontent over segregation and discrimination.

In that the President called the attention of the grave challenge which lies before it and spelled out the obligation and responsibility involved.

Among the highlights, the President summoned both parties to the common responsibility of equality in opportunity, in education and the right to work.

Hamlett Chapel Marks Men's Day On Sunday; Bishop Smith, Speaker

The Chapel C. M. E. Church located 2510 Coward Street will celebrate its Men's Day Sunday June 23, 1963. Rev. Turner, assistant pastor, will deliver the morning message.

At 3:00 P. M. the Bishop B. Julian Smith of Chicago, Illinois will be guest speaker. The public is cordially invited to worship with us and help make this a great day for our men. Rev. A. L. Brown, pastor, Bro. Earl Martin, Chairman, Rev. Robert Palmer, Co-chairman.

White Student Breaks Barrier At ALA. A. & M.

HUNTSVILLE, Ala. —(ANP)— While Gov. George C. Wallace of Alabama was busy making a grand stand play to the nation Tuesday by standing in the doorway of the University of Alabama, a white student was quietly integrating a Negro college in the state for the first time.

The desegregation of Alabama A and M, which happened by accident, occured when Robert Muckel, who is white, was accepted at the school and learned that it was Negro after he arrived in the campus.

Muckel, 29, said that he planned to stay at the college. He is a chemistry teacher from Utica, Neb., and filed application to six colleges under a summer program run by the National Science Foundation.

Muckel said he learned that the school was all-Negro when he attempted to get housing accommodations for his wife.

The campus is approximately five-miles from the University of Alabama where two Negroes were enrolled this week under federalized national guardsmen.

School officials said that Mr. Muckel was the first white student knowingly admitted to the school since it was founded in 1875.

"Everyone has been exceptionally nice to me. They've gone out of their way to make me feel at home," Mr. Muckel said.

Leaders Agree To Set Up U. S. Rights Committee

Not Bar Life, Ju

By LOUIS CASSELS

WASHINGTON — (UP) —Supreme Court justices went to unusual lengths Monday to make clear that they were not barred from public life when they ruled that it is unconstitutional for public schools to hold exercises.

The court's long + searching was clear and unequivocal, saying that devotional prayer and Bible readings have no place in public schools. On that both text one of the nine justices were in emphatic agreement.

The most striking dissenting opinion was by Justice Potter Stewart.

But the majority opinion, written by Justice Tom Clark, of its way to emphasize that all right for schools to teach religion and to use the Bible as a source book in teaching.

"It might well be said that ...

United C Synod To

NEW YORK. — The General Synod of the United Church of Christ, meeting in December 4-11, has set aside large time to wrestle with the problem of religion and race, and its influence on peace and the relationship of government to freedom and welfare.

The 700 synod delegates representing two million member denominations will consider a proposal by the United Church Board for Homeland Ministries for a $1,000,000 grass to expand and implement the Church's work in race which began in 1846.

The Board now supports many accredited universities and in the South, founded long after the Civil War for Negroes.

Gettys Dedica

GETTYSBURG, PA. — In a wreath + laying ceremony Saturday, dedication of the century commemorative stamp, installation of additional battle markers and an address by Pennsylvania Governor William W. Scranton.

4 • CHATTANOOGA OBSERVER • Friday, June 7, 1963

CHATTANOOGA OBSERVER

Published Every Friday at 208 East Ninth Street
Chattanooga, Tennessee
BY THE NEGRO NEWS PUBLISHING COMPANY

WALTER C. ROBINSON .... Manager

SUBSCRIPTION RATES
1 Year—$3.12   6 Months—$1.60   3 Months—85 Cents
Ten Cents Per Copy

Telephone AM 6-4061   P. O. Box 292

Entered as Second-class Mail Matter February, 1935 at U. S. Post-
office, Chattanooga, Tennessee.

Dr. Archibald Carey, Jr. and George W. Brooks Commencement Speakers Challenge Many

The seventy-seventh commencement exercise of Howard High School held Friday evening, May 31st at Memorial Auditorium was a thrilling and challenging farewell for 325 graduates.

Developing the theme, "Education, The Gateway To Freedom And Democracy" were Eleanor Ruth Hines, salutatorian; Audrey Jean Roberts, valedictorian; and Dr. Archibald Carey, Jr., minister of Quinn Chapel A.M.E. Church, Attorney and Counsellor of Chicago, Illinois who used as his subject "One Hundred Years After."

Comparing educationally the Negroes plight one hundred years ago on "Emancipation Day" — when only about one out of a hundred could read or write with the present picture of thousands graduating from high school and colleges today.

Economically, his plight was very poor — turned loose with no home, land, money or skill, but today the picture is brighter with promises of future brilliance.

During this one hundred years of progress much work, thought and service has been wrought under pressure until today our "Civil Rights" fight is a direct aftermath. Eloquently discussing both the debit and credit freedom fight ledger, he then said, "The Negro is saying to the world through sit-ins, stand-ins and pray-ins that complete freedom is our only salvation and security — that is "freedom of opportunity." After the opportunity is given it will be up to the Negro to make it a sound investment."

Excerpts from his speech, which drew thunderous applause, were such pointed statements as: "What people are expected to repeat daily, the pledge of Allegiance to the flag of the United States and sing America without it someday becoming a reality"

.... "Why go half way around the world to shout freedom, if you can't even say it softly in Birmingham" .... "Kill a Negro leader today and 1,000 more will rise up" .... In answer to the numerous inquiries about the "Master Plan Headquarters" — "there is no headquarters — the plan is in the heart and mind of every pressured Negro. In answer to What does the Negro want? — "The Negro wants what every other person, regardless of race, wants in America, "Equal Opportunity and Equal Justice."

The twenty-eighth commencement exercises of Booker T. Washington High School held Thursday evening in the school gymnasium was a challenge to 38 graduates.

Developing the theme: "The Achievement of Equality Through Quality" were Patricia Ann Witherow, salutatorian; Lena Faye Smith, valedictorian; Paul Hickman, faculty representative and Mr. George Brooks, principal of Burt High School, Clarksville, Tennessee, who used as his subject "Rights and Responsibilities of Graduates Today."

He said, "Graduates, your responsibility is to grow up and become good citizens and it is your rightful duty to return to society as compensation of what has been done for you." Humor...

Zion Commencement
(Continued from Page One)

and Mrs. Rosa Carter. The general public is cordially invited to attend these exercises.

U. Of Georgia
(Continued from Page One)

it too thin, he said.

He asked the graduates to justify the sacrifice of their families and friends by making a contribution to society and making this a better day through their devotion to Georgia.

Following the main assembly of all of the graduates on the field of the stadium, where they marched to receive their diplomas from the Deans of their respective schools, there was the usual rush of parents and friends to offer their congratulations. Miss Hunter and Mr. Holmes received best wishes from some of their white classmates.

Holmes, who made the Phi Beta Kappa honor society will be the first Negro student enrolled at the Emory University, School of Medicine in Atlanta comes September. Meanwhile he will return to his old job as life guard at Washington Park during the summer.

Miss Hunter, who is now on a week's vacation out of the city, will begin duties as a staff member of the New Yorker magazine sometime next week.

Thus ended the Charlayne Hunter and Hamilton Holmes' University of Georgia story. As full bona-fide graduates they now join the more than 48,000 alumni. Although they are not the first Negroes to graduate from the University of Georgia they are the most celebrated and heralded.

Miss Mary Francis Early, a music teacher in the Atlanta public school system received a Master degree in Music from the University of Georgia last summer.

Four other Negroes finished their freshman year there this past school year. They are: Harold Black, Mary Blackwell, Karen Robin, and Alice Henderson, all of Atlanta.

Rev. Robinson To
(Continued from Page One)

in the Emanuel Baptist Church of this city, and will be remembered for his spiritual deliverance in song, prayer and sermon.

Services will begin nightly at 7:30 o'clock. Remember, the series of services will begin June 10th, and conclude June 16th. Rev. J. Q. Mileage is pastor of Emanuel.

Bro. Joe May
(Continued from Page One)

gain the opportunity for education. He said "The Lord has blessed me and by singing, I have been able to to educate my children. So it gives me great joy to sing in support of Zion College.

Kennedy To Dese

WASHINGTON

...bill— barring dis-
...struction programs
of workers or oppre...

President institutes in the South administration move t... tary desegregation of ... industries.

The President issued statement asserting discontent among Negroes problems in every country.

He met later in t... 300 prominent busine...

He said these prob... met partly by his program but that he using his new anti-d... directive and taking steps to end job discrimination in this country.

The new anti-discrimination order would cover fair construction as well as civil building.

In announcing his nedy said he was dissatisfied Willard W...

Robinson's newspaper was a weekly paper distributed on Thursdays. He hired a secretary, photographer, advertising agent, and a man to be in charge of the circulation of the paper. Thursday's paper would contain news of the previous weekend plus news of the early part of the current week—Monday, Tuesday, and Wednesday. Robinson worked very hard with the necessities of making the paper a prosperous business as well as making it interesting to readers.

Robinson, after becoming the owner of the *Chattanooga Observer*, continued to be very active in politics. He remained chairman of the Fourth Ward until 1959 when urban renewal split up the ward. Even he had to move along with a great many of the supporters. But he was consistently elected chairman of the Colored Voters League of Greater Chattanooga until his death.[60] This attested to his great talent for leadership and the desire of the people to be led by him.

The *Chattanooga Observer* was published and circulated on somewhat a small scale from 1933 to 1935, but when Robinson resigned as truant officer for the Chattanooga Public School System in 1935, he then devoted his energies fully to his newspaper as his chief source of livelihood.[61]

Robinson worked very hard to ensure the success of his business. His political affiliations proved to be beneficial to his newspaper business. He asked politicians that he supported to do certain things for the benefit of his business once they were in office. Following is a letter written to P. R. Olgiati, mayor of Chattanooga, on August 19, 1955.

Dear Mr. Mayor:

I am in need of a few more regular advertisers. I note that Furlow-Cate Ford Dealers advertise regularly in the daily papers, along with several other automobile dealers. I thought maybe that you might have some friends in some of those organizations that might give us, say $5 or $10 worth of advertising a week. That's not much but it will help out with what we have.

Since our advertising program with the Electric Power Board never did materialize as you and I thought it would, or as they promised you and me it would. Knowing the city of Chattanooga buys a lot of materials, automobiles and what not from various firms, if you would speak to the right parties about some advertising for the Observer, it will help me greatly.

Thanks for the consideration you will give the aforementioned request.

I remain
Your Sincere well-wisher
The Chattanooga Observer
/s
Walter C. Robinson, Publisher

Walter Robinson also intended to use his newspaper as an instrument to support the Republican Party. As mentioned before, he strongly believed in the Republican Party and felt that many black citizens could be reached through his newspaper. He wrote all the editorials for his paper, which usually concerned politics. Robinson also wrote editorials, which concerned race problems, and he wrote on any subject that was controversial at the time.[62]

To give you an example of Robinson's efforts for the Republican Party and his style of writing, the writer will here include a portion of one of his editorials.

Support Governor Alfred M. Landon, Republican Candidate for President of the United States. Governor Landon made a good start in his several addresses the past few days as he opened his campaign in the East. To the radio audience, accustomed as it has been to the glamorous radio voice of President Roosevelt, here was a new type of radio personality, not possessed of a particularly forceful radio voice, but a man whose sincerity rings true by his words.[63]

Robinson often asked candidates that he supported for political advertisements for his newspaper. Following is such an inquiry to E. D. Crump, dated July 27, 1942.

The Honorable E. D. Crump
Memphis, Tennessee

Dear Sir:

Taking note of your many insertions in the many papers of our state, and being the only colored newspaper of our city and county, we feel almost obligated to ask for some sort of advertisement to help fill in our paper on July 31, as we will be carrying political ads for others.

As we pride ourselves in always caring for those interested in politics, our rates are fifty cents per column.

Just notify us as to your matter to be run, or we will pick up anything you have run in other papers. We are sending you under separate cover, one of our copies. All news for publication must be in this office not later than Wednesday at five P.M.

Mr. Walter C. Robinson,
Owner and Manager
Rev. L. J. Flemester,
Advertising manager

P. S. For your benefit, take note of our strength politically speaking, before you form your decision.

As can be noted from the above letters, Robinson worked hard to make his business successful. He used every means to get his paper known and respected as well as circulated over a wide area.

The *Chattanooga Observer* contained almost every phase of news. Most often, the headlines concerned major activities of a church group, such as AME'S IN ANNUAL MEET AT ST. PAUL NOV. 1-5. The next major column would concern news items of national importance. The remainder of the paper included almost all categories of news, such as world, state, national, regional, church, civic organizations, gossip, community, women, society, health, sports, and advertisements.[64]

COUNTY COUNCIL MAN AND
J. P. CANDIDATES CHECK
STRATEGY LIST

CHATTANOOGA OBSERVER ★ Thursday, March 9, 1967

MARION
JACKSON
Views
Sports of The World

EDITOR'S NOTE—Sports Editor Marion E. Jackson is confined to bed at home and today's column is by staff writer James D. Heath.

(World Sports Staff)
Chicago Bears All-Pro defensive back Roosevelt Taylor plans to retire . . . Six ton basketball players were named to Look All-America Team . . . In another NFL story, San Francisco 49ers' QB John Brodie has already been traded to the New York Giants . . . Savannah must be a basketball city, the Central of Georgia Railroad added several cars to the Nancy Hanks, to bring the Beach High Bulldog fans to Atlanta for the GHSA State AAA Tournament . . .

LEAVING THE WINDY CITY — All - Pro defensive back Roosevelt Taylor of the Chicago Bears is leaving the windy city. Taylor plans to retire from pro football and return to New Orleans because the cold weather is affecting the health of his young daughter.

Daytona Pit Crews Also Win Top Recognition

DAYTONA BEACH, Fla. — Last Saturday's Permatex 300 - mile race for sportsman and modified stock cars was won by Jim Paschal.

S. C. State To Represen' SIAC In NCAA Tou: ney

ORANGEBURG, South Carolina — South Carolina State College Bulldogs will represent the Southern Intercollegiate Athletic Conference (SIAC) in the NCAA Mideast - South Central Regional Tournament (College Division) in Evansville, Indiana on March 9-11.

WILLIE, YOU FORGOT Willie Mays drews th ASTROJET GOLF CLA

Panthers Set For

Carver
19 An(

There were several sources of news items. The paper subscribed to the regular national newspaper network and the various black colleges, social, and civic clubs. Churches and community representatives mailed or brought news items to the newspaper office.[65]

One of Robinson's main objectives for his newspaper was to rebuild his image to the public and to strip McMillan of his job as commissioner of education. Robinson commenced immediately upon resigning from the Chattanooga School System as truant officer to attack McMillan through his editorials. McMillan's attempts to fire black city employees, especially teachers and janitors who were friends of Robinson's, was his first mistake. The black citizens realized that some of the people attacked were of the most respected and qualified to do their jobs.[66] It became obvious that McMillan was not really concerned that black children receive an equal education but rather that McMillan was just another prejudiced white man who could not bear the idea of a black man having as much power as did Walter Caldwell Robinson. It was upsetting to McMillan to see a black man occupy an office in city hall and act as a white man wearing a suit, walking with his head held high, speaking correct English when talking to white people, and looking them in the eyes during a period when segregation and discrimination were at their peaks in Chattanooga, Tennessee.[67]

Robinson used his paper to make black citizens aware of McMillan's aims at splitting the black citizens, thus breaking up the political strength they held as a united group. He wrote editorial after editorial until his respect was regained. Most understood McMillan's evil tactics.

The next local election proved that Robinson had been successful. Robinson supported R. M. Cooke in the next local election, and Cooke won by a landslide because of the black votes.[68]

Walter Caldwell Robinson had plenty reason to be satisfied with himself. The goals of his paper were attained in less than ten years. Black citizens were responding to his paper, and many of those who in the past had not become concerned enough about the community problems or politics to attend the meetings began to show interest because of Walter's newspaper. He was successful in getting McMillan out of office in the very next election. Also, Robinson's business had become quite prosperous. In 1943, his paper was being circulated throughout Hamilton and surrounding counties. There were subscriptions from many former Chattanoogans in every state of the union and some foreign countries. By 1943, Robinson was ordering over 3,500 papers weekly.

The newspaper business continued to prosper, and the *Chattanooga Observer* was published thirty-five consecutive years.

Thursday, September 12, 1968, should have been declared a day of mourning in the black communities of Chattanooga, Tennessee. This day marked the ending of a great black citizen. A citizen who was unusual in many respects, a man among men, a father, husband, politician, Christian, businessman, leader, and humanitarian.

The following letter, page 64, marked the end of the *Chattanooga Observer*.

THE CHATTANOOGA OBSERVER

A Weekly Newspaper With A Constructive Policy

208 East Ninth Street—P. O. Box 293

Telephone 266-6043 or 266-1473

Chattanooga, Tennessee 37403

Walter C. Robinson, Sr., Publisher

Mrs. Cora B. Robinson, Managing Editor

October 4, 1968

Dear Subscriber and Advertiser:

It has been a joy to serve you with weekly issues of the *Chattanooga Observer*. Because of thoughtful people like you, the *Observer* has had thirty-five (35) years of continuous service.

Thursday, September 12, 1968 at 6:45 p.m. marked the passing of Publisher Walter C. Robinson, Sr., and with his passing the *Chattanooga Observer* marked its final run for 1968. We, the family, regret the loss of both.

Your kindness and understanding in the past will sustain and help us chart our future course.

May God bless and keep you; looking always toward a brighter tomorrow.

Respectfully yours,
/s
(Mrs.) Cora B. Robinson
Editor
/s
Marian R. Robinson, Manager
1008 Oak Street

LUB EWS

East Chattanooga News

CHURCH NEWS

Lookout Mountain, Tennessee.

Personal

Army Not To Show Race Designations

Ike Takes Oath On Bible Given Him By Mother

Court Says Ala. U. Not In Contempt

16-Year-Old Boy Confesses Slaying

"With God

Another Candidate Eliminated From Judgeship Post

SPORTS OF THE WORLD
BY MARION E. JACKSON

100% Wrong Club Jamboree To Attract Top U. S. Stars

Global Sports Stars To Come To Atlanta For All-Sports Fete

Alcorn Braves Top Southern Cats 65-63

Florida A & M Tops Tuskegee 85 To 56

Metropolitan Atlanta High School Round-Up
By Joel W. Smith

Clark Panthers Sweep To 82-63 Win Over S. C. State Bulldogs
Teody Wright Steals Spotlight With 35; James Enoch Gets 14
By Joel W. Smith

BAMBOO CURTAIN IS NO ROCK 'N-ROLL BARRIER

Alabama A & M Cagers Win Over Knoxville

51

Same Rights Bill From Last Year

BILL PASSED HOUSE BUT GOT STALLED IN SENATE

SUNDAY SCHOOL LESSON

Prime Minister Resigns Post In Eastern Nigeria

Expert On Rights Named To Jewish Congress

CHAPTER V

Summary

The life of Walter Caldwell Robinson is an inspiration to blacks because it is the story of a black man struggling throughout his life to uplift his race. Robinson was born the son of sharecroppers in Larkinsville, Alabama, on July 17, 1893. His family lived in Alabama and worked the farm of a white man until Walter was nine years old.

Walter's parents, Joseph and Elizabeth Robinson, decided to move to Chattanooga, Tennessee, when he was nine, seeking better employment and educational opportunities for their children. In Chattanooga, their economic status improved, but due to segregation and discrimination, their plight was yet very bleak. In spite of these despairing circumstances, the children—Floyd, Monroe, Jessie, Rosa, Fannie, Amanda, and Walter Caldwell Robinson—were able to lift themselves to a higher level of participation in a tightly segregated society.

Walter showed signs of a businessman and leader at an early age. At age 11, he secured employment in a foundry and, by age 16, was operating a laundry business of his own.

Walter Robinson married one of his neighbors and classmate, Cora Adair. To this marriage were born seven children: Evelyn, Marian, Walter Jr., Jessell, Camille, Lucille, and Alma Lee.

Religion was an important aspect of a black man's life during this period in Chattanooga, Tennessee; therefore Walter, Cora, and their children were very active members of the Second Missionary Baptist Church. Robinson became president of the Baptist Young People's Union soon after joining the church in his youth. At age 21, he became a trustee of the church. Robinson was an asset to the church because he was able to influence outstanding ministers to accept the pastorship of the church when the church was without a minister. After becoming a politician, he was able to raise large sums of money for church undertakings by asking wealthy whites that he had come in contact with for donations.

Robinson began attending the meetings of his ward (Fourth Ward). Because of the interest he exhibited in ward, local, and national politics and his leadership ability, he was elected chairman of this ward, defeating Hiram Tyree, who had been ward leader many years. Walter was very successful in creating interest and participation among black citizens.

In a short while, Walter's influence spread throughout Chattanooga and Hamilton County because he organized the chairmen of all the black wards and established the Colored Voters League of Greater Chattanooga for the purpose of getting recognition for blacks through a united group.

In 1926, Robinson was selected to conduct a campaign tour of northern and northwestern states by the National Republican Executive Committee. In his addresses, he encouraged blacks to support the Republican candidates for president, vice president, and for Congress because he felt that this was the best avenue for ending segregation and discrimination.

Because of his political involvements, he was chosen to be an alternate delegate to the Republican National Convention in Kansas City, Missouri, for the first time in 1928. He was an alternate delegate at each National Republican Convention thereafter until his health failed in 1963.

H. D. Huffacker was supported by Walter Robinson and the Colored Voters League of Greater Chattanooga for the position of commissioner of education in 1927. Huffacker was elected and, once in office, gave Robinson a job as a truant officer for the Chattanooga Public School System. He was responsible for seeing that black boys and girls attend school, but because of his power and leadership ability, he was given the responsibility of suggesting blacks to be hired as teachers, janitors, and in other departments of the city. Robinson worked in this capacity until a candidate that he opposed was elected commissioner of education in 1935.

Upon resigning as a truant officer in 1935, Robinson began working full-time for the success of his newspaper business, which he started in 1933. This newspaper, the *Chattanooga Observer*, was initiated for the purpose of expressing his views to benefit the Republican Party and to defeat candidates in local elections who Robinson felt were not the best candidates for the good of the black citizens and for the purpose of enlightening and uniting the black citizens of the Chattanooga area.

Robinson was continually elected chairman of the Fourth Ward until urban renewal split the ward in 1959. He was continually elected chairman of the Colored Voters League of Greater Chattanooga until his death. His newspaper, a thirty-five-year venture, was published from 1933 until his death in 1968.

Walter Caldwell Robinson was a black man who possessed an unusual propensity for achievement. He emerged as a leader in his community, and through the power that he gained by organizing the masses of blacks, many achievements were made. He was successful in securing jobs for his followers, recognition and representation in politics, and spent the majority of his life striving to help blacks attain power as well as first-class citizenship.

APPENDICES

DIRECTORY OF APPENDICES

Appendix A

WALTER C. ROBINSON
THE CHATTANOOGA OBSERVER
POST OFFICE BOX 293
CHATTANOOGA, TENNESSEE

December 10, 1956
Sheriff V. W. Maddox
Hamilton County Jail
Walnut Street
Chattanooga, Tenn.

Dear Sheriff:

The bearer of this note is Fletcher Little of 945 Taft Street in Park City. He is a friend of ours and has done a good job in helping our cause all over the city and particularly in Park City.

He served Commissioner McInturff as special police at Lincoln Park last summer and did a good job out there. He is interested in a deputy sheriff commission. He says he has his bond made with Felix Diamond. I understand that he is not interested in using it to go out fee grabbing but there may be some dances he might want to police.

I am sure he is a good risk and if you will give him a commission I will appreciate it. Incidentally, the Voters League organization unanimously endorses him for a commission.

Respectfully,

/s

Walter C. Robinson

WCR:1s

Appendix B

WALTER C. ROBINSON
THE CHATTANOOGA OBSERVER
POST OFFICE BOX 293
CHATTANOOGA, TENNESSEE
October 1, 1956

Mr. L. H. Templeton
Supt. of Streets
Chattanooga, Tenn.

Dear Mr. Templeton:

The bearer of this note is Benjamin Patterson of 1005 Cedar St., Third Ward. He is out of work and claims to be a good worker and will work if given an opportunity to do so.

He was recommended to me by Mr. Barnes of the Engineering Department of Public Works. He said he has worked for him on the yard and impresses him as being a good worker. Since I only sent you one last week and I understand he quit, which was as I expected, please put on this man. I understand he is a real hard worker. He is married and needs a job. If you will help him I will appreciate it.

I understand Robert Baxter has laid off so soon, so put this man in his place and if he comes back, just let him continue to stay off. If he is no more interested in the job than to lay off so soon, there is no point in fooling with him.

Thanks for the consideration you will show this man. I remain

Very truly yours
/s
Walter C. Robinson

Appendix C

WALTER C. ROBINSON
THE CHATTANOOGA OBSERVER
POST OFFICE BOX 293
CHATTANOOGA, TENNESSEE
26 September 1956

Mr. Ernest Robinson
3767-18th St.
Ecorse, Mich.

Dear Uncle Ernest:

I conveyed to your brother, Uncle T, through letter immediately after I arrived home, how well you are getting along there in Ecorse. I haven't been able to run down to Scottsboro due to the fact that I have been unusually busy in this Eisenhower campaign.

I hope your family is getting along nicely. My family is okay with the exception of my wife, who is suffering with a cold, but that is to be expected. I hope you are doing everything possible to help Eisenhower there in your hometown, because if he is not elected I am sure the Negroes' cause in the South will suffer greatly. I think it is the duty of the Negroes in the North and East who are allowed to vote to vote to help their brothers in the deep South since millions of them can not vote.

For example, your brother, Uncle T. cannot vote on election day. The Democrats do not allow Negroes to vote without a lot of red tape attached to it in Alabama. So when you go to vote, stick in one for Eisenhower and you will be helping your brother in Alabama and all the other relatives all over the South. It is the Democratic party that is against the Negro all over the country and particularly in the South where a majority of the Negroes live. I talked with Herbert Tucker the day before I left there and he said he was voting the Republican ticket straight and was doing everything he could to get others to do the same.

Thanks for the interest that you and your family manifested in me while I was in your city. Give my regards to your family and the other people that I met while at your home. I remain

Yours for Republican Success in November
/s
Walter C. Robinson
WCR:1s

Appendix D

WALTER C. ROBINSON
THE CHATTANOOGA OBSERVER
POST OFFICE BOX 293
CHATTANOOGA, TENNESSEE
15 October 1956

Mrs. Rosa Thompson
621 E. Secons St.
Muncie, Ind.

Dear Sister Rosa:

Finding that my itinerary will bring me close to you on October 25th which is Thursday of next week, I thought maybe some of the kids or some of the people that came from Muncie to hear me a few years ago would like to know about it. If so, I would be glad to see them. My schedule is so congested I am not sure I will be able to run over to see you. If some of the kids should come over, I would be happy to see them.

I am working my heart out for Eisenhower and Nixon and the Republican ticket generally. I am sure you will vote Republican as you were raised that way.

The address in Anderson, Indiana as I said will be October 25th at 7:30 p.m. at the Hazelwood School auditorium and in Richmond, Indiana on the next night, which is October 26th and from there, I am not sure. I will be glad to see anyone from your town.

Hope your family and you are feeling well. My family here is okay including Amanda. However Charles has not been too well for the past couple of weeks or more. This is all for now. I remain

Your Brother,
Walter C. Robinson
WCR/1s

Appendix E

ADDRESS DELIVERED BY WALTER C. ROBINSON
RICHMOND, INDIANA
October 26, 1956
THE RE-ELECTION OF EISENHOWER AND NIXON AND A
REPUBLICAN CONGRESS IS THE ONLY HOPE FOR
NEGROES TO BECOME FIRST CLASS CITIZENS
IN THE UNITED STATES OF AMERICA

Mr. Chairman, and fellow Americans, it is good to be back in the great Republican State of Indiana to commune with you on the eve of this national election. As a citizen of Chattanooga, Tennessee, the home city and state of the Democratic nominee for Vice President, Senator Kefauver, I have elected to talk to you from a subject that I think is of great importance, not only to the Negroes of America, but the American people in general. Thus my subject, "THE RE-ELECTION OF DWIGHT DAVID EISENHOWER AND RICHARD NIXON AND A REPUBLICAN CONGRESS IS THE ONLY HOPE FOR NEGROES TO BECOME FIRST-CLASS CITIZENS IN THE UNITED STATES OF AMERICA."

The choice between Eisenhower-Nixon and Stevenson-Kefauver must be made on November 6, 1956. Millions of American citizens will march to the polls on the date above mentioned to make their decision at the ballot box. But unfortunately, there are millions of Negroes in the deep south that will be prohibited from Participating in this all-American election because the Democratic party, who dominates and controls all of the southern states, and particularly those of the deep south, refused to permit Negroes to vote. Not by law, but by intimidation and intimidation is worse than by law. Therefore the Democratic party must, and rightly so, be charged with taking from millions of Negroes in the deep south their inalienable rights to cast their ballot unmolested and undisturbed. Thus, no party is good enough to be given the authority to preside over the greatest nation in all the world, the United States of America, who takes from loyal citizens their right to participate in their government through the intimidation right.

The Democratic party is a party of disfranchisement, discrimination, and segregation and no party is entitled to be honored with the leadership of this nation who has built a reputation as a party who sponsors, believes, and advocates segregation, discrimination, and non-compliance with the laws of the nation as enunciated by the Justices of the Supreme Court of the United States.

Stevenson and Kefauver's party believes in just that. The recent shameful investigation of the public schools of the District of Columbia is a product of the Democratic Party, in that, they sponsored it and they must assume the credit for it. The 84th Democratic controlled Congress authorized the investigation in Washington. The 84th Democratic Congress appropriated the money to do the investigating with and they appointed as investigators men from the deep south whose attitudes toward members of the darker races are extremely bad. And to be sure they could give integrationists a black eye, they selected a smear artist, Mr. Gerber, of Memphis, Tenn., my state, as chief counsellor for the investigators.

Thus, the Democratic Party, the party of Stevenson and Kefauver, must assume the full credit for the shameful investigation of the schools in the District of Columbia. And any party that would condescent to such depths to destroy the hope of Negroes and their children in this country is not fit to lead this great American nation.

The recent disclosure of bills enacted into law in Virginia is an evidence of what the Stevenson-Kefauver party thinks of Negroes in America. Many of the bills passed were fantastic, they condescended to an all-time low to make law for Virginia that would destroy the hope and aspiration of Negroes for all times to come. And, in view of the close alliance of southern manifesto signers to the high command of the Democratic party, gives Negroes to know that the Democratic high command could not be trusted to defend their interests if and when needed. The Democratic high command, or the candidates for President and Vice President on the Democratic ticket, held several regional meetings shortly after the nominational conventions closed. One of those meetings was held in Knoxville, Tenn, where Mr. Stevenson and Kefauver presided, and the type of people that were invited to that meeting by Governor Stevenson and Senator Kefauver were people who are enthusiastically opposed to all civil rights for American Negroes in this country. Not only are they opposed to it but they have publicly stated their position. Such men as the Senators from Mississippi, Eastland and Stennis; Talmadge and Russell of Georgia; Hill of Alabama, Fulbright of Arkansas; Ellender of Louisiana, and many others like them were there. They came out of the huddle after the conference and each of them was singing the same theme song, "we are for Stevenson and Kefauver." No Negroes were invited to the conference and there were none there, therefore we cannot say what the big agreement was, but we do know the type of men that attended the conference and their attitudes toward Negroes. Therefore we are convinced that Stevenson and Kefauver, the Democratic standard bearers, appeased those men by telling them something that all of them agreed to since each and all of them are enthusiastically supporting the Democratic ticket for President and Vice-President.

Eisenhower and Nixon

Approximately four years ago the American people were disturbed, bewildered, and many of them discouraged because of the situation they were in at that time.

The patron saint of the Fair Deal, Mr. Truman, had sent the Americans across the Sea to Fight in Korea without authority from the Congress of the United States. Mothers were receiving sad news daily that their sons or husbands were missing in action. The prayer was for someone to rescue America from the clutches of the Democratic party or maybe the Fair Deal party.

Dwight David, Eisenhower heard the call and responded. A few short months after his inauguration as president, the Korean War came to a dramatic end and the American boys were returned home to be reunited with their families to the delight of millions of American mothers.

The thinking of the Democratic high command for twenty long years had been that we must have war to make for prosperity. Eisenhower showed America and the world that that was a misnomer—that you did not have to have war to enjoy peace and prosperity and as a result, the Eisenhower Administration has ushered in the greatest peacetime prosperity in the history of our nation. More than 66 million people are working and their take-home pay is the highest in history. Thus we can, with justification, state that the Eisenhower-Nixon Administration has been one of service and outstanding accomplishments to the people of this great nation.

Indianians should be happy about that record because many of your illustrious sons, such as your brilliant U. S. Senator Capehart, Congressmen John Beamer, and others, participated in the Eisenhower program. Therefore they are entitled to their share of the credit for this peace and prosperity that we are enjoying in America today.

Since Eisenhower and Nixon's Administration has meant so much for the good of America, it appears that Americans would be ingrates if they failed to endorse, at the polls, their successful efforts. It has been the policy down across the years, and especially in politics, to give a public official who has made good, an endorsement of his record at the polls and I believe you are going to do just that this year.

I am here from the south, a border state, Tennessee. Four years ago we put Tennessee in the Eisenhower column, in that the Tennessee electoral votes went along with others to swell the tide that swept a great and beloved president into office. We are fighting the good fight again. We feel that we have an opportunity to duplicate what we did in '52 and we are much encouraged at this moment.

But Negroes from the deep south sent me here to beg of you, since they cannot vote on election day, prevented from doing so by the Democratic party, to vote for them and I don't think they are asking too much of you. Many of you are familiar with the conditions under which they live, and intimidation will keep them from doing in the deep south what you will be doing here in free Indiana on election day, that is vote. They asked me further to say to you to repudiate by driving out of office and keeping others from coming into office, those of the Democratic faith who have held them in semi-slavery down through the years.

Negroes Earned Right to First Class Citizenship

I think the Negro's loyalty and patriotism to the Flag of our country, since before the immortal Lincoln signed his Emancipation Proclamation, in all wars entitles him to be classified and given rights of first-class citizen. Eisenhower has attempted to do just that, in that he has cleaned up the mess in Washington. He has integrated restaurants, hotels, transportation carriers and everything else he could possibly do to make Democracy work in the District of Columbia. He has been fair with all of the people. He said the ruling of the Supreme Court of the United States, as it relates to schools in '54, was the law of the nation and as President, he is sworn to uphold the law.

The only logical way we have of judging the future is by the past. The only way that we can say what you will do is by what you have done. Eisenhower showed an interest in all the people of the nation, irrespective of religion, race, or national origin.

We are predicting that he will do it again. Thus the hope of the Negro people in America is the Re-election of Eisenhower and Nixon and the election of a Republican Congress. And if I don't misunderstand the signs of the time, as I traverse this country, I have faith to believe that the people will give Eisenhower and Nixon a new lease on the political life by re-electing them by an overwhelming majority on November 6th.

Appendix F

CHARTER OF COLORED VOTERS LEAGUE
OF GREATER CHATTANOOGA
Preamble

Whereas one of our most blessed privileges as American Citizens in the State of Tennessee is our right of suffrage, and

Whereas through various means too numerous to mention, we as a people have become educated up to the importance of Organization, and

Whereas the trend of public welfare seem to depend partly if not wholly so, upon political influence based upon voting strength; We therefore resolve to band ourselves together hoping to get what recognition we may, enabling us to be of greater service to ourselves and automatically to our people throughout greater Chattanooga; We this Committee have drafted for you consideration, the following instrument designated to be the governing document of our proposed Organization.

The object and purpose of this Organization is to inculcate and foster in the minds of its members, and the public generally the importance of using their god given rights to cast a ballot in all Elections. To teach obedience to law and order, to disseminate patriotism and loyalty to the government of the City, County and several states of the United States and to assist our race in securing all of the rights and privileges that other citizens of the United States enjoy.

Constitution

Article I—Name

This Organization shall be known as "The Colored Voters League of Greater Chattanooga."

Article II—Officers

The officers of this Organization shall be, Chairman, Vice-chairman, Recording Secretary, Assistant Secretary, Treasurer, and Chaplain.

Article III—Duties

The duties of the officers shall be the same as those performed by officers of any well organized deliberative assembly. The Chairman to preside over all meetings in his absence however, the Vice-chairman shall occupy the chair, etc.

Article IV—Elections

The officers of this organization shall be elected annually, subject to re-election. Such elections to be held the first meeting in October.

Article V—Executive Committee

The Executive Committee shall consist of five members. Our Chairman by virture of his position shall be Chairman of said Committee, the other four members to be elected by the body.

Article VI—Membership

Any legal voter of our race from whichever ward or precinct within the city of Chattanooga is eligible to membership, however application for membership must be approved by the body.

Article VII—Restriction of Membership

Any number of voters may be admitted to membership in this organization, but no ward or precinct shall have more than five votes.

Article VIII—Penalty

A member of this organization revealing any of our proceedings to a non-member of this body, candidates especially, shall be suspended. However the right of appeal before the executive committee shall not be denied the member. The verdict of said committee to be final.

By Laws

Section I

Article I

Amendment

The constitution may be amended as often as the body deem necessary, provided written notice to that effect be given at least thirty days prior to such action. Two-thirds of the votes present being necessary to amend the constitution.

Article II
Quorum

Five (5) members representing as many wards of precinct at any one meeting, shall constitute a Quorum.

Article III

Schedule Day, Time and Place of Meetings

The organization is to meet semi-monthly, subject to calls for extra sessions as our Chairman deems necessary, on such day and time agreed upon by the body. The place of meeting to be designated by our Chairman from time to time until a permanent place is provided for our meetings.

Article IV
Rule of Order

Robert's Rule of Order shall be our guide and the order of business left with the descretion of the presiding officer.

Respectfully submitted,

/s

R. W. Allen, Chairman
Sidney H. Byers
Rev. A. Johnson
Ernest Horton
H. Hogarth, Sec't
Done in the City of
Chattanooga, State of Tennessee;
this 9th day of September in the
year of our Lord 1930.

Appendix G

ADDRESS DELIVERED BY WALTER C. ROBINSON
AT THE SPRUCE ST. BAPTIST CHURCH
FEBRUARY 16, 1958—3 PM
MASS ACTION WITH THE BALLOT IN HIS HAND
IS THE WAY OUT FOR NEGROES

Mr. Master of Ceremonies, Officers and Members of the sponsoring organization, Ladies and Gentlemen:

It's an honor to have been invited here to commune with you on this history making occasion. I understand today climaxes your week of activities as it relates to Negro History Week. I am sure Dr. Eppse, one of the outstanding authorities on history in America as one of your sponsors of this program has been a great asset to you.

You are sponsoring your program this year at a time when Negroes are going through one of the darkest periods in his history. The forces of darkness, led by irresponsible and uninformed people, have set up road blocks of hate to prevent the clear passage of Negroes from second class to first-class citizenship. Especially is this true since the '54-'55 decisions of the Supreme Court of the United States. But Negroes are determined to become first class citizens in these United States of America. It can be done, it should be done, and it will be done providing that Negroes mass their action carrying with them their greatest protection, the ballot. Thus, my subject is Mass Action with a Ballot in His Hand Is the Way Out for Negroes.

There are many Negro leaders who differ in their procedure as it relates to the best means of achieving his ultimate goal. But I am thoroughly convinced that mass action on the part of Negroes with a ballot in his hand is his way out. The ballot is the most powerful instrument that he can use to gain for himself the right to be respected as a first-class citizen. You cannot win this fight for freedom with sticks, and rocks, and guns, but you can win it with the ballot. Some people respect religion, but all people respect power.

Since the passage of the Civil Rights Bill by the Congress of the United States guaranteeing the protection of Negroes' rights as it relates to voting, Negroes in various parts of the country, particularly in the south, are re-doubling their efforts to increase their voting strength, and rightly so. If the prediction of some of the Negro leaders who are taking a lead in the fight to increase Negro vote power is accurate, approximately one-half million more Negroes' names will find their way to the registration lists all over the southland.

But to increase that vote strength you will have to do it over the opposition of many people in our southland. The Associated Press reported only last week that the Governor of Georgia is planning to resort to the old trick of requiring a poll tax as a prerequisite for voting, and I understand he will call upon the legislature of Georgia to restore that feature as a voting privilege in his state of Georgia.

He may be able to restore the poll tax as a voting privilege, but that's somewhat doubtful because the Congress of the United States has said, in their recent Civil Rights Bill, that every American should be protected in his right to cast his ballot according to the dictates of his own conscience. Therefore Negroes should put forth every effort to register and vote this year and every election thereafter.

The ballot is more powerful than the sword and if the Negro would win his freedom, or a free right to be enumerated with other first-class-citizens, he must go to the polls and register and vote. My suggestion is that it should be done in mass. Minority groups cannot afford to scatter their shots, they cannot afford to divide for when they divide they lose their effectiveness.

Many people have solved and are solving their problems through mass action. Industry is solving its problems through mass production; labor unions are solving their problems through mass organization; the Jewish people are solving their problems through mass action. Since they are solving their problems as above mentioned, it is reasonable to believe that minority groups like Negroes can solve their problems through mass action with the ballot in their hands. The Jewish people, a minority in America, through mass action have built for themselves a financial empire and the Jewish financiers of America, through massing their action, can underwrite the financial program of the United States. Our hope lies in mass action with ballots in our hands. You cannot win this fight, and I repeat for the sake of emphasis, with sticks, rocks and guns, but you can win the fight by mass action with ballots.

The American Negro has always had a tough, rugged road to travel since his emancipation 90 odd years ago. Immediately after the immortal Lincoln wrote the Emancipation Proclamation he (the Negro) was subjected to problems apparently too large to overcome. The first problem he was called upon to solve was the problem of living side by side with his former masters in peace. He solved that problem, in that he achieved something that no other racial group has been able to do. The American Indians tried it and the streets were drenched with blood. But the Negro, through common sense and with a prayer on his lips, has been able to grow from four million to approximately 16 million living side by side with those who held him as slaves.

The next great problem he was forced to solve was to find a way to secure sufficient foods to keep soul and body together since when he was emancipated he had no money in the bank, in the creek or anywhere else and but a few friends. But he solved that problem, and today there are thousands of fertile farms owned and operated by Negroes throughout the southland.

The next problem he was called upon to solve was to find a way to educate his children. With a determination to see his offspring acquire an education, he started on his way and today, Negroes by the thousands possess every type of degree which says that he has successfully passed the examinations required by the Boards of Education throughout the nation and particularly the South.

The Negroes of yesteryears solved their problems by mass action and common sense and it is the duty and responsibility of Negroes of today to solve their problems. It must be done by mass action on the part of Negroes with the ballot in their hands.

Appendix H

DR. EPPSE WILL DELIVER THE LINCOLN-DOUGLAS BIRTHDAY CELEBRATION ADDRESS AT FRIENDSHIP BAPTIST CHURCH ON GROVE STREET SUNDAY, FEBRUARY 10 AT 3 PM

Prof. Merle R. Eppse, director of history and geography at A. & I. State University, Nashville, outstanding authority on Negro history, Elk, and Mason, will deliver the principal address for the Lincoln-Douglas birthday celebration at the Greater Friendship Primitive Baptist Church, 117 Grove Street, Sunday, February 10, at 3 p.m.

The celebration is sponsored annually by the Colored Voters League of Greater Chattanooga, many outstanding speakers have been brought to Chattanooga to appear on these programs.

Mrs. Alma Battle, wife of the pastor of First Baptist Church, E. Eighth Street, will read the life of Frederick Douglass. Mrs. Jessie C, Bonam, city school teacher, will read the life of Abraham Lincoln. The Elks Marching Units will serve as ushers. Miss Edna M. Thomas and Mr. Marvin Montgomery will be soloists for the occasion and the Number One Crack Choir of Friendship Church will furnish music.

The sponsoring organization is urging and inviting all Chattanoogans to participate in these celebrations. Remember the program begins promptly at 3 p.m. February 10.

Appendix I

2707 Wood Avenue
Chattanooga, Tenn.
Nov. 11, 1953
Honorable W. T.
Judge of Hamilton County
Court House
Chattanooga, Tenn.

Dear Judge:

I am taking this method to thank you and the county manager for straighting out the streets in Bozentown, the colored people who have tried for years to get something done for those streets, are elated over your preformance. As a leader of that precinct for a number of years, I think that I can afford to say that I am speaking the sentiment of all the colored people in that area and we stand ready and willing to do anything that you want done that we can do at any time. Thanks again.

I remain yours truly,

Appendix J

Colored Voters League of Greater
Chattanooga
124½ East Ninth Street
Chattanooga, Tennessee
October 3, 1952

Honorable P. R. Olgiati
Mayor of Chattanooga
City Hall
Chattanooga, Tenn.

Dear Mayor:

In keeping with a resolution unanimously adopted in a semi-monthly meeting the Colored Voters League of Greater Chattanooga Thursday, October 3, 1952, as it relates to the woman police traffic officers at crossings near schools are being used to a good advantage in many cities throughout the nation, and two in Tennessee, namely, Memphis and Nashville we feel that the experiment should be tried here.

The recommendation by the Commissioner of Fire and Police that he be allowed to employ 20 women to be used at crossings near school at a cost of $50 per month and purchase other regalia needed by the officers is sound and reasonable. We understand that the women police officers are paid $60 per month in Nashville and the city purchases their equipment.

Since more automobiles are being put in service on the streets of Chattanooga daily, and many of them manned by amateur drivers, it makes the traffic problem in Chattanooga increasingly more dangerous and, in view of the fact that crime, according to a national report is on an increase throughout the nation and according to our best information, there is a shortage of policemen in Chattanooga as it relates to the national requirement, we feel that to release the police that are making $310 per month from traffic duty at school crossings and employ others at $50 per month the city would be practicing strick economy and yet giving the people the type protection needed.

Therefore, in view of the fact that you, as Mayor of Chattanooga and whose duty it is to look out for the general welfare of the same, we are urging that you give this proposition of employing women for traffic duties around school buildings serious consideration, and, if possible, find sufficient money to finance the proposition and instruct the Commissioner of Fire and Police to proceed with lightning speed to employ the 20 women for traffic duties in Chattanooga.

Respectfully,
Colored Voters League of Chattanooga
Walter C. Robinson, President
Prof. J. W. Williams, Secretary
Eugene Hyatt, Treasurer
Rev. C. B. Holloway, Chaplain

cc to:
Commissioners:
George McInturff
Pat Wilcox
Frank Trotter
Roy Hyatt

Appendix K

Chattanooga, Tennessee
————1934

Dear Sir:

For more than fifty years the colored citizens of Tennessee, have adhered to the principles, upheld the policies, and supported the nominees of the Republican party. They have done all of this with only a small voice in the councils and management of the party's affairs. We feel that the Negroes of this section, and, especially, of the third congressional district, due to the large vote given to the party nominees each year, deserve representation on the state Republican Executive Committee. We are therefore, offering the name of Walter C. Robinson, for election to that post in the coming, August contest.

Walter C. Robinson, has given twenty years of service to the Republican Party. He has served for twelve years as chairman of the Fourth Ward of Chattanooga. He has represented the party on the state and national movements. Under his leadership the Fourth Ward has lead all other voting precincts in Hamilton county for the past ten years. He is honest, capable and trustworthy; and if elected, as we think he should be, he will do more, and work harder to build up the Republican Party, than any man whom we know in this district.

Trusting that you will give your wholehearted support to the election of a deserving republican to a place on the state Republican Executive Committee. We remain yours,

Respectfully,

Robert B. Buckner
Dr. E. F. McIntosh
Dr. Leroy Capehart
Rev. John M. Miles
Rev. N. B. Morton

Appendix L

WALTER C. ROBINSON
THE CHATTANOOGA OBSERVER
POST OFFICE BOX 293
CHATTANOOGA, TENN.
8 July 1955

Dr. W. S. Davis
President of A&I State University
Nashville, Tenn.

Dear Dr. Davis:

I haven't had time to let you know how much we appreciated your visit to Chattanooga and at the Second Baptist Church recently. It made me very happy because of the tremendous turnout that greeted you and the fine address you gave the people. They are still talking about it and few people that have been to Chattanooga has been acclaimed like you were when here. Accept my thanks for your coming.

I know you have a thousand and one different things to think about and to do, but I am using this method to call your attention to one James Henry Pressley who has made application to attend your school this fall. This is the boy that I had his parents to speak to you when you were here. The boy is very anxious to get an education and his father is not so well and financially is not able to pay a full tuition. He is interested in some work at the university to help him out. Any type of work, washing dishes, digging ditches, anything, he will work. I will appreciate it if you will consider him for work and let me know. Too, his mother informed me that she is not sure whether he will be able to stay on the campus. I know the congestion you must have in the way of students, I know also of the limited campus space you have. But if you could arrange to do those two things for him, his parents and I will appreciate it.

Thanks again for coming to Chattanooga. I hope in the future you will scrouge in enough space to see us again. I remain

Your Sincere Well Wisher
/s
Walter C. Robinson
WCR:1S

Appendix M

SECOND BAPTIST CHURCH
1348-50 Grove Street
Chattanooga, Tenn.
March 27, 1956

Mr. Harry Carbaugh, President
Tennessee Egg Company
414 W. 16th Street
Chattanooga, Tenn.

Dear Mr. President

I want to thank you for your liberal donation in connection with a special effort sponsored by our church that terminated March 25th. The donation was made through our member and trustee, Brother Walter C. Robinson. It is men like you that makes life worth living.

Our drive was a tremendous success and Robinson, who was one of the captains, made a very fine showing in that direction.

We have purchased a brand new bus to transport Sunday School children and the older people to and from church.

Again, I want to thank you for the officers, members and friends of the Second Baptist Church for your liberal donation.

Very truly yours,
Rev. M. H. Ribbins, Pastor
MHR:1s

Appendix N

TENNESSEE
AGRICULTURAL & INDUSTRIAL
STATE COLLEGE
William J. Hale, President
NASHVILLE
September 13
1933

Mr. Walter Robinson
City Hall
Chattanooga, Tenn.

My dear Mr. Robinson:

Miss Jacola Foust, the daughter of Rev. Brown, I understand is teaching temporarily at Main Street School.

Her record with us is good. If you can consistently have her retained as a teacher I am sure you will make no mistake in securing the services of this young woman.

Yours very truly,
W. J. Hale, President
WJH:EJV

Appendix O

GIVE COLORED CHILDREN SQUARE DEAL SAYS McMILLAN

Chattanooga's colored children deserve to be taught correctly just the same as white children and to have teachers of good reputation who live up to the same high standards of purity as white teachers, Commissioner T. H. McMillan said yesterday when pressed for a statement as to the behind the scenes story of the Paralee Shropshire case.

That's the basis of my effort to retire Paralee Shropshire and some other colored teachers from the school system, the commissioner continued, and charges that my actions are prompted by any other motive are unqualifiedly and maliciously false.

I am trying to get a square deal for the colored children of Chattanooga and it makes my blood boil when somebody begins to shout "politics" because of the teachers I would release chance to be friends of Walter Robinson. Walter picked some teachers of the wrong type and it's those who are marked for the discard, not because they happen to be friends of Walter.

I have kept dozens of janitors and scores of teachers who got their jobs from Robinson. I have retained every one of his appointees who is giving good service. I don't desire to tear the colored part of the system all to pieces and I have not taken action against a single teacher until I felt that I was sure of my ground.[69]

Appendix P

Appendix Q

Obsequies
of
MR. WALTER C. ROBINSON, SR.
Editor: THE CHATTANOOGA OBSERVER

Second Missionary Baptist Church
1348 GROVE STREET
Chattanooga, Tennessee

Sunday, September 15, 1968—1:15 PM
REV. PAUL A. McDANIEL, Officiating

FRANKLIN-STRICKLAND FUNERAL HOME
In Charge

Mr. Walter C. Robinson, Sr. was born July 17, 1893 in Larkinsville, Ala. He was one of seven children of the late Mr. and Mrs. Joseph Robinson. He departed this life Thursday, September 12, 1968 at 6:45 PM.

His family moved to the city of Chattanooga, Tennessee, when he was seven years of age. He attended the public schools here. He was united in Holy Matrimony to Miss Cora B. Adair in the year of 1914 and to this union seven children were born. Six children survive his passing.

He accepted Christ under the pastorate of the late Rev. J. H. Mastin and joined the Second Missionary Baptist Church, which was his wife's church home. He became a Trustee and was instrumental in helping to locate the church at its present site. He remained a dutiful and dedicated member.

Mr. Robinson was noted for his oratorical ability and became known as and billed: "The Silver-tongued Orator." He was often called upon by many local, state and national organizations and churches to speak on auspicious occasions. He early knew the power of the vote, in helping a struggling people and so, for a quarter or more of a century, lent his efforts in this struggle. He worked with the Republican Party and served many terms as Vice Chairman of the Hamilton County Republican Executive Committee and Chairman of the "powerful" 4th Ward. Mr. Robinson was an alternate delegate to several Republican National Conventions. He organized and served as President of the Voters' League of Greater Chattanooga until his health failed.

Thirty-five years ago, he became editor of the *Chattanooga Observer* newspaper and served in this capacity until his passing.

The deceased is survived by his wife, Mrs. Cora Adair Robinson; five daughters, Mesdames Evelyn Hardin, Alma Poole, and Lucille Blakemore; Misses Marian and Camille Robinson; one son, Walter C. Robinson, Jr.; one sister, Mrs. Amanda Kelley, one granddaughter, Miss Sandra Hardin; one grandson, Master Harris Adair Robinson; one uncle, Mr. Ernest Robinson; three sons-in-law, Mr. George S. Hardin, Mr. Donnell Blakemore, and Mr. Haywood Poole; one daughter-in-law, Mrs. Truly Robinson; also nieces, nephews, cousins and many dear friends.

ORDER OF SERVICE

ORGAN PRELUDE
PROCESSIONAL
SONG Choir
"Come Ye Disconsolate"
SCRIPTURE and PRAYER Rev. Louis Brooks
SOLO Mrs. Lila Sammons
"Someone to Care"
RESOLUTIONS
REMARKS:
Rev. H. H. Battle
Rev. C. B. Holloway
Mr. Louis Young
Atty. F. Todd Meacham
Mr. Fred Hixson
Mr. James Culberson
SOLO (Family Request) Mr. Claude Finley
"Standing on the Banks of Jordan"
ACKNOWLEDGEMENTS Mrs. Loretta Stuart
OBITUARY (Read Silently) with Soft Music
THE EULOGY Rev. Paul A. McDaniel
RECESSIONAL—Mortician in charge
INTERMENT—FOREST HILLS CEMETERY

THANKS

The family of the late Walter C. Robinson, Sr. wishes to express sincere thanks to everyone for their expressions of sympathy.

For every floral design, telegram, card, visit and other kindnessess, we are grateful.

May God bless each of you.

—The Family

Blessed are the dead which dieth in the Lord; yea they shall rest from their labors, and their works do follow them.

ACTIVE PALLBEARERS	FLOWER ATTENDANTS
Askew, Charles	Askew, Jimmie
Culberson, James	Coleman, Emzie
Cooper, Early	Freeman, Essie
Freeman, Moses	Green, LaFrieda
Farrow, Will	Green, Mattie
Jackson, Andrew	Hicks, Jessie
Sanders, James	Kennebrew, Elizabeth
Traughber, Charles	Palmer, LaVesta

HONORARY PALLBEARERS

Official Board of Second Baptist

Cope, Joseph	Jarrett, Jehu
Alford, John	Scott, Nathan
Thomas, James	

BIBLIOGRAPHY

Newspapers

Chattanooga Times, March 11, 1928.

Chattanooga Times, April 22, 1933.

Chattanooga Times, March 9, 1934.

Chattanooga News Press, August 12, 1932.

Chattanooga Times, February 13, 1933.

Chattanooga Times, May 8, 1933

Chattanooga Times, September 30, 1933.

Chattanooga Times, March 24, 1933.

Chattanooga Times, May 18, 1933.

Chattanooga Times, October 9, 1933.

Chattanooga Times, March 13, 1935.

Chattanooga Times, April 2, 1935.

Chattanooga Times, April 8, 1935.

Chattanooga Times, September 8, 1935.

Chattanooga Times, June 22, 1938.

Chattanooga Times, May 16, 1938.

Chattanooga Defender, April 18, 1930.

The *Chattanooga Observer,* September 4, 1936.

Chattanooga Times, September 30, 1936.

Documents

Charter. "Colored Voters League of Greater Chattanooga." Chattanooga, Tennessee. September 9, 1930.

Taped Interviews

Evelyn Hardin, daughter of Walter C. Robinson. Chattanooga, Tennessee. April 12, 1974.

J. H. Harris, deacon of Second Missionary Baptist Church. Chattanooga, Tennessee. March 7, 1974.

Emery Henderson, vice chairman of the Colored Voters League of Greater Chattanooga, 1940-42. Chattanooga, Tennessee. March 5, 1974.

Cora Robinson, wife of Walter C. Robinson. Chattanooga, Tennessee. April 12, 1974.

Marian Robinson, daughter of Walter C. Robinson. Chattanooga, Tennessee. April 12, 1974.

Peter D. Simmons, photographer for the *Chattanooga Observer.* Chattanooga, Tennessee. April 14, 1974.

James Skillern, vice chairman of the Colored Voters League of Greater Chattanooga, 1935-38. Chattanooga, Tennessee. March 9, 1974.

Alma Spence, teacher, friend, and neighbor of Walter C. Robinson. Chattanooga, Tennessee. March 2, 1974.

Letters

Carter, Mary L. to Walter C. Robinson. November 11, 1934.

Colored Voters League of Greater Chattanooga to Governor Frank Clement. February 25, 1953.

Colored Voters League of Greater Chattanooga to Mayor P. R. Olgiati. October 3, 1952.

Colored Voters League of Greater Chattanooga to chairman of the State Republican Executive Committee. 1934.

Hale, W. J. to Walter C. Robinson. September 13, 1933.

Ribbins, M. H. to Mr. Harry Carbaugh. March 27, 1956.

Robinson, Cora B. and Robinson, Marian Robinson to subscribers and advertisers. October 4, 1968.

Robinson, Walter C. to Sheriff V. W. Maddox. December 10, 1956.

Robinson, Walter C. to Mr. L. H. Templeton. October 1, 1965.

Robinson, Walter C. to Mr. Ernest Robinson. September 26, 1964.

Robinson, Walter C. to Mrs. Rosa Thompson. October 15, 1956.

Robinson, Walter C. to Judge W. T. Thrasher. November 11, 1953.

Robinson, Walter C. to Dr. Walter S. Davis. December 30, 1953.

Robinson, Walter C. to Commissioner W. E. Wilkerson. March 29, 1935.

Robinson, Walter C. to Mayor P. R. Olgiati. August 19, 1955.

Robinson, Walter C. to E. D. Crump. July 27, 1942.

References Consulted

Franklin, John Hope. *From Slavery to Freedom*. New York: Knopf, 1974.

Green, Lorenzo J., and Carter G. Woodson. *The Negro Wage Earner*. New York: AMS Press, 1970.

Quarles, Benjamin. *The Negro in the Making of America*. New York: Macmillan Company, 1969.

Scott, Mingo Jr. The Negro in Tennessee Politics and Governmental Affairs. Nashville: Rich Company, 1964.

ILLUSTRATIONS

ILLUSTRATION I

(*Reading from left to right*) Dr. Merle R. Eppse and Walter Caldwell Robinson.\

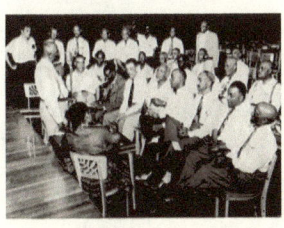

ILLUSTRATION II

Walter C. Robinson (*standing*) organizing Republican Club for the purpose of securing jobs for blacks in Nashville, Tennessee\

ILLUSTRATION III

Black newspaper publishers' meeting in mid-'50s—Atlanta, Georgia
(*Second from left*) Walter C. Robinson; (*seventh from left back row*) Benjamin Mays, president of Morehouse College

WALTER CALDWELL ROBINSON: PRESIDENT AN LORD OF BLACK CHATTANOOGA

AN ABSTRACT

The contributions made by Walter Caldwell Robinson certainly deserve to be recorded and passed on to future generations. He played a very vital role in the black man's struggle in his city, state, and the nation. Robinson was responsible for lessening the burdens of thousands of black Americans and spent the majority of his life doing what often was thought impossible to get recognition and acceptance for his people as humans and first-class citizens.

Walter was born the son of sharecroppers in Larkinsville, Alabama, on July 17, 1893. His family lived in Alabama and worked the farm of a white man until Walter was nine years old.

Walter's parents, Joseph and Elizabeth Robinson, decided to move to Chattanooga, Tennessee, when he was nine, seeking better employment and educational opportunities for their children. In Chattanooga their economic status improved, but due to segregation and discrimination, their "plight" was yet very bleak. In spite of these despairing circumstances, the children, Floyd, Monroe, Jessie, Rosa, Fannie, Amanda, and Walter C. Robinson, were able to lift themselves to a higher level of participation in a tightly segregated society.

Robinson showed signs of a businessman and leader at an early age. At age 11, he secured employment in a foundry and, by age 16, was operating a laundry business of his own.

Walter Robinson married one of his neighbors and classmates, Cora Adair. To this marriage was born seven children: Evelyn, Marian, Walter Jr., Jessell, Camille, Lucille, and Alma Lee.

Religion was an important aspect of a black man's life during this period in Chattanooga, Tennessee; therefore Walter, Cora, and their children were very active members of the Second Missionary Baptist Church. Robinson became president of the Baptist Young People's Union soon after joining the church in his youth.

At age 21, he became a trustee of his church. Robinson was an asset to the church because he was able to influence outstanding ministers to accept the pastorship of the church when the church was without a minister, and after becoming a politician, he was able to raise large sums of money for religious undertakings by asking wealthy whites that he had come in contact with for donations.

Walter began attending the meetings of his Fourth Ward. Because of the interest he exhibited in ward, local, and national politics and his leadership ability, he was elected chairman of this ward defeating Hiram Tyree, who had been ward leader for many years. Walter was very successful in creating interest and participation among black citizens.

In a short while, Walter's influence spread throughout Chattanooga and Hamilton County because he organized the chairmen of all the black wards and established the Colored Voters League of Greater Chattanooga for the purpose of getting recognition for blacks through a united group.

In 1926, Robinson was selected to conduct a campaign tour of northern and northwestern states by the National Republican Executive Committee. In his addresses he encouraged blacks to support the Republican candidates for president, vice president, and for Congress because he felt that this was the best avenue for ending segregation and discrimination.

Because of his political involvements, he was chosen to be an alternate delegate to the Republican National Convention in Kansas City, Missouri, for the first time in 1928. Thereafter he was an alternate delegate at each National Republican Convention until his health failed in 1963.

H. D. Huffacker was supported by Walter Robinson and the Colored Voters League of Greater Chattanooga for the position of Commissioner of Education in 1927. Huffacker was elected and, once in office, gave Robinson a job as a truant officer for the Chattanooga Public School System. He was responsible for seeing that black boys and girls would attend school, but because of his power and leadership ability, he was given the responsibility of suggesting blacks to be hired as teachers, janitors, and in other departments of the city. Robinson worked in this capacity until a candidate that he opposed was elected commissioner of education in 1935.

Upon resigning as a truant officer in 1935, Robinson began working full-time for the success of his newspaper business that he started in 1933. This newspaper (*The Chattanooga Observer*) was initiated for the purpose of expressing his views to benefit the Republican Party and to defeat candidates in local elections whom Robinson felt were not the best candidates for the good of the black citizens and for the purpose of enlightening and united the black citizens of the Chattanooga area.

Robinson was continually elected chairman of the Fourth Ward until urban renewal split the ward in 1959. He was also continually elected chairman of the Colored Voters League of Greater Chattanooga until his death. His newspaper, a thirty-five-year venture was published from 1933 until his death in 1968.

Walter Caldwell Robinson was a black man who possessed an unusual propensity for achievement. He emerged as a leader in his community and, through the power that he gained, organized the masses of blacks and realized many achievements. He was successful in securing jobs for his followers, as well as recognition and representation in politics, and spent the majority of his life striving to help blacks attain power and first-class citizenship.

The period in which Robinson struggled was indeed challenging. The masses of black people during the 1920s-1950s in Chattanooga, Tennessee, were of the lowest socioeconomic status and possessed little educational training. Robinson organized blacks and spoke with power to whites because of his support from the black masses. He printed in his newspaper evils that were placed on blacks by whites and openly fought discrimination, segregation, and prejudice during a period when intimidation, that would lead to lynching, were about as common as prayer meetings and the Ku Klux Klan was as revered by whites in the South as a religion.

This great American would probably be forgotten in a few years if this study had not been undertaken. The writer is quite pleased to have had a part in capturing the activities of this outstanding leader, politician, and businessman so that present and future citizens may profit from the contribution he made in Tennessee.

It was the purpose of this study to describe the life and activities of Walter Caldwell Robinson from 1893 to 1968. More specifically, it was the aim of this study to give an account of Robinson's early life as a farm boy in Alabama and in the ghetto of Chattanooga, Tennessee; to describe his efforts and successes in obtaining financial security; to present his activities as a politician, although he was never elected to a political office; to explain his contributions as a newspaper publisher and editor; and finally to summarize his major activities and contributions in his profession in a time when Blacks were legally out of the accepted political arena.

This study is important because, to this date, nothing in the form of a biography or any other work has been written about this great citizen of Tennessee. This great American made life a little easier for blacks in Chattanooga as well as other areas of Tennessee and the nation. He organized black people for the purpose of electing white officials who would be considerate of the black man's problems. Believing that voting was the only sensible means of getting recognition during his time, Robinson put this means into action, and many accomplishments were made.

This study is biographical in nature, but political and business aspects are considered as they relate to the activities in which he was a part. Chattanooga, Tennessee, is the primary location but other states and cities are mentioned as they relate to Robinson's activities.

The writer obtained data for this investigation primarily from the morgue and library of the *Chattanooga Times* and the *Chattanooga Free Press*. Taped interviews with Robinson's relatives and associates proved to be most beneficial. Thus on the whole, original and primary sources were used and interpreted.

Malcolm J. Walker

Biography

He graduated from Booker T. Washington High School in 1964. Malcolm sent himself to college and completed requirements for the bachelor of science degree in history at Tennessee State University in Nashville, Tennessee, in 1968. He earned the master of science degree in history from Tennessee State University in 1971.

Malcolm was employed by the Chattanooga Public Schools in 1968. He worked as a classroom teacher, assistant principal, supervisor, and director before retiring after thirty-three years of service in 2001.

Malcolm loves to travel and has explored five of the seven continents. He continues to make Chattanooga his home.

SUMMARY OF THE LIFE OF WALTER CALDWELL ROBINSON

"Get some sense in your head, some God in your heart, some money in your pocket, and a ballot in your hand!" This was a message by Walter Caldwell Robinson, who became known as the Silver-tongued Orator as he traveled the country, making speeches to black audiences for the National Republican Committee beginning in 1926.

Walter C. Robinson was born the son of sharecroppers in Larkinsville, Alabama, in 1893. His family moved to Chattanooga, Tennessee, when he was nine years old. At age 11, Walter worked a part-time job in a foundry each morning before going to school. By age 16, he was operating a laundry business of his own. Walter married his childhood sweetheart and fathered seven children. By age 21, he was a trustee in the Second Missionary Baptist Church.

Walter became interested in politics and was elected chairman of the powerful Fourth Ward—the largest black voting precinct in Chattanooga at the time. He eventually organized all the chairmen of black wards and formed the Colored Voters League of Greater Chattanooga. The league became so powerful that it could determine winners in local elections. Walter was chosen alternate delegate to the Republican National Convention each election from 1928 to 1963.

Walter C. Robinson and the Colored Voters League supported H. D. Huffacker for commissioner of education in 1927. Huffacker won and gave Robinson a job as a truant officer for the Chattanooga Public School System. His office was located in city hall. Robinson's power and duties extended far beyond keeping black boys and girls in school. The hiring of teachers, janitors, and cooks in the black schools was determined by Robinson. He also recommended the filling of positions in other departments of the city. Robinson worked in this capacity until a candidate that he opposed was elected commissioner of education in 1935.

In 1933, Walter began publishing a black weekly newspaper: the *Chattanooga Observer*. It was the purpose of his newspaper to express his views to benefit the Republican Party, to defeat candidates in local elections felt by Robinson not to be in the best interest of black citizens, and for the purpose of enlightening and unifying the black community.

Walter continued to be elected chairman of the Fourth Ward until 1959. He served as chairman of the Colored Voters League until his death. He published the *Observer* for thirty-five years—from 1933 to 1968.

Walter Caldwell Robinson was a successful businessman, an outstanding orator, an astute politician, and a powerful leader. He labored in segregated Chattanooga during a time when the Ku Klux Klan was as revered as religion.

ENDNOTES

1 Taped interview with Mrs. Cora Robinson (wife of Walter Caldwell Robinson), Chattanooga, Tennessee, April 12, 1974.

2 *Chattanooga Times*, March 11, 1928, p. 3.

3 Taped interview with Mrs. Cora Robinson (wife of Walter Caldwell Robinson), Chattanooga, Tennessee, April 12, 1974.

4 Ibid.

5 See appendices A and B.

6 *Chattanooga Times*, April 22, 1933, p. 4.

7 See appendices C and D.

8 See appendix E.

9 *Chattanooga Times*, April 22, 1933, p. 4.

10 Ibid.

11 See appendix F.

12 See appendix G.

13 *Chattanooga Times*, March 9, 1934, p. 7.

14 Taped interview with Mr. James Skillern (vice chairman of the Colored Voters League of Greater Chattanooga, 1935-38), Chattanooga, Tennessee, March 9, 1974.

15 Ibid.

16 See appendix H.

17 Taped interview with Mr. Emery Henderson (vice chairman of the Colored Voters League of Greater Chattanooga, 1940-42), Chattanooga, Tennessee, March 5, 1974.

18 See appendix H.

19 *Chattanooga News Press*, August 12, 1932, p. 2.

20 See appendix J.

21 See appendix K.

22 See appendix L.

23 Taped interview with Mr. J. H. Harris (deacon of Second Missionary Baptist

Church), Chattanooga, Tennessee, March 7, 1974.

24 See appendix M.

25 Taped interview with Mr. J. H. Harris (deacon of Second Missionary Baptist Church), Chattanooga, Tennessee, March 7, 1974.

26 Taped interview with Mrs. Alma Spence (teacher, friend, and neighbor of Walter Caldwell Robinson), Chattanooga, Tennessee, March 2, 1974.

27 See appendix N.

28 *Chattanooga Times*, February 13, 1933, p. 3.

29 Ibid.

30 Ibid.

31 *Chattanooga Times*, May 8, 1933, p. 5.

32 Ibid.

33 *Chattanooga Times*, September 30, 1933, p. 2.

34 *Chattanooga Times*, March 24, 1933, p. 6.

35 Ibid.

36 *Chattanooga Times*, May 18, 1933, p. 4.

37 *Chattanooga Times*, October 7, 1933, p. 4.

38 Ibid.

39 Ibid.

40 Ibid.

41 *Chattanooga Times*, October 9, 1933, p. 2.

42 *Chattanooga Times*, March 13, 1935, p. 2.

43 See Appendix O.

44 *Chattanooga Times*, April 2, 1935, p. 2.

45 *Chattanooga Times*, April 8, 1935, p. 4.

46 See Appendix P.

47 *Chattanooga Times*, September 8, 1935, p. 5.

48 Ibid.

49 Ibid.

50 *Chattanooga Times*, June 22, 1938, p. 6.

51 *Chattanooga Times*, May 16, 1938, p. 2.

52 Ibid.

53 Taped interview with Ms. Marian Robinson (daughter of Walter Caldwell Robinson), Chattanooga, Tennessee, April 12, 1974.

54 Taped interview with Mrs. Cora Robinson (wife of Walter Caldwell Robinson), Chattanooga, Tennessee, April 12, 1974.

55 *Chattanooga Defender*, April 18, 1930, p. 1.

56 Ibid.

57 Letter to Walter C. Robinson from Scott Newspaper Syndicate, March 12, 1943.

58 Ibid.

59 Ibid.

60 Taped interview with Mrs. Cora Robinson (wife of Walter Caldwell), Chattanooga, Tennessee, April 12, 1974.

61 Ibid.

62 Taped interview with Peter D. Simmons (photographer for the *Chattanooga Observer*), April 14, 1974.

63 The *Chattanooga Observer*, September 4, 1936, p. 8.

64 Ibid.

65 Ibid., Taped interview, Peter D. Simmons.

66 Taped interview with Ms. Marian Robinson (daughter of Walter Caldwell Robinson), Chattanooga, Tennessee, April 12, 1974.

67 *Chattanooga Times*, September 30, 1935, p. 6.

68 Taped interview with Mrs. Evelyn Hardin (daughter of Walter Caldwell Robinson), Chattanooga, Tennessee, April 12, 1974.

69 *Chattanooga Free Press*, September 26, 1935, p. 1.

www.ingramcontent.com/pod-product-compliance
Lightning Source LLC
Chambersburg PA
CBHW021121130626
46554CB00002B/812